教材编写组

主 编：周 婷

编 委：宋文杰　李 俊　胡逸舟　周献德
　　　　涂 纳　刘蔚然　刘 蕊　李 红

插 图：陈超清

江西省汉语国际推广项目资助

这里是江西

文化篇

周 婷 ⊙ 主编

图书在版编目（CIP）数据

这里是江西.文化篇/周婷主编.－－南昌：江西人民出版社，2023.8
ISBN 978-7-210-14753-4

Ⅰ.①这… Ⅱ.①周… Ⅲ.①汉语—对外汉语教学—教材②地方文化—江西 Ⅳ.① H195.3 ② G127.56
中国国家版本馆CIP数据核字（2023）第124913号

这里是江西·文化篇
ZHELI SHI JIANGXI · WENHUA PIAN

周　婷　主编

责 任 编 辑：何　方
装 帧 设 计：同异文化传媒

出版发行

| 地　　　址：江西省南昌市三经路47号附1号（330006）
| 网　　　址：www.jxpph.com
| 电 子 信 箱：jxpph@tom.com
| 编辑部电话：0791-86898846
| 发行部电话：0791-86898815
| 承　印　厂：南昌市印刷十二厂有限公司
| 经　　　销：各地新华书店

开　　本：787毫米×1092毫米　1/16
印　　张：9.5
字　　数：220千字
版　　次：2023年8月第1版
印　　次：2023年8月第1次印刷
书　　号：ISBN 978-7-210-14753-4
定　　价：68.00元
赣版权登字－01-2023-288

版权所有　侵权必究
赣人版图书凡属印刷、装订错误，请随时与江西人民出版社联系调换。
服务电话：0791-86898820

编写说明

《这里是江西：文化篇》是《这里是江西》系列汉语文化教材的第二册。此系列教材以汉语文化夏令营及其他短期来赣外国团组或个人为目标对象，模拟外国人士在江西学习和生活的真实场景，巧妙融合了赣鄱文化元素，形成了独具特色的内容体系。本书在编写的过程中力求遵循如下原则：

一、语言为主、融合文化

作为《这里是江西》系列教材的文化篇，本书把课文场景设定为江西历史文化名胜，把独具特色的赣鄱文化有关内容巧妙融入对外汉语语言教学之中。本书共10个单元，内容涉及江西美食文化、江西瓷文化、江西茶文化、江西戏曲文化、江西书院文化、江西中药文化、赣南客家文化等文化专题，介绍了景德镇、滕王阁、庐山、八大山人等江西具有标志性的文化名片。让学习者在学习汉语语言知识的同时，也能对江西深厚的文化有所了解，达到语言学习与文化学习相统一的目的。

二、循序渐进、突出文化

本书语言知识点的选取编写建立在第一册的基础上，篇章结构延续第一本的主要框架，分为热身、课文、生词、语法、练习和文化贴士六个主要部分。相较于第一册侧重于基础汉语知识，本册的热身部分以文化知识导入的形式，突出了赣鄱文化元素。课文分为 A 和 B 两个部分，课文篇幅较第一本有明显加长，句式更为复杂，生词量也有所增加。语言知识点的安排注重先后顺序，达到循序渐进的效果。每课之后的文化贴士部分参考相关研究成果进行撰写，旨在向读者更深入、更全面地介绍江西特色文化，激发学生进一步阅读和了解江西文化的兴趣。

三、侧重听说、兼顾读写

本书的编写侧重学生汉语听说技能的提升和对赣鄱文化知识的普及宣传。课程设计注重实用性较强的听说训练，强调语言应用的交际场景，让学习者在短时间内快速掌握常用表达、语言点以及其对应的交际场景，提高学生实际语言应用能力。

本教材可供短期来赣外国团组、个人汉语学习以及集中强化培训使用，教师可根据实际教学情况采取机动灵活的方式安排授课内容。编写组在教材编写过程中参考了有关文献，在此我们表示衷心的感谢。教材几经修改，若有错漏之处，诚望大家提出宝贵意见。

编写委员会
2022 年 12 月

目录
CONTENTS

第一课　你吃过江西菜吗？	/ 01
LESSON 1　Have you ever had Jiangxi cuisine?	

第二课　我一次景德镇都没去过 .... / 13
LESSON 2　I have never been to Jingdezhen City

第三课　滕王阁有多高？ .... / 25
LESSON 3　How tall is the Tengwang Pavilion?

第四课　文港毛笔历史真悠久 .... / 39
LESSON 4　The history of Wengang writing brush is really long

第五课　我一边喝茶一边欣赏庐山美景 .... / 53
LESSON 5　I enjoyed the beautiful scenery of Mount Lushan while drinking tea

第六课　江西的戏曲越听越好听 .... / 65
LESSON 6　The more I listen to Jiangxi opera, the better it sounds

第七课　我把八大山人纪念馆逛完了 .... / 77
LESSON 7　I finished visiting the Badashanren Memorial Hall

第八课　白鹿洞书院有一千年左右的历史 .... / 91
LESSON 8　Bailudong Academy has a history of about one thousand years

第九课　樟树的中药多极了！ .... / 105
LESSON 9　Zhangshu has many traditional Chinese medicines!

第十课　我被客家文化吸引了 .... / 119
LESSON 10　I am attracted by Hakka culture

生词总表 .... / 133
Vocabulary

参考书目 .... / 144
Bibliography

本书人物
CHARACTERS

Wáng Yuè
王 月
Wang Yue

Jiāng Nán
江 南
Jiang Nan

Lǐ Yáng
李 阳
Li Yang

Pí'āi'ěr
皮埃尔
Pierre

Héxī
荷西
Jose

Měinà
美娜
Mena

第一课　你吃过江西菜吗？
LESSON 1　Have you ever had Jiangxi cuisine?

- 知识目标：掌握"过""有点儿"的用法
- 能力目标：能够用汉语点菜
- 文化目标：了解江西饮食文化

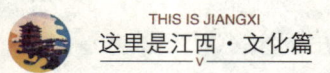

第一课　你吃过江西菜吗？

Key Sentences
重点句　Zhòngdiǎn jù

1. 你吃过江西菜吗？　　　　　　Nǐ chīguo Jiāngxīcài ma?
2. 我有点儿饿。　　　　　　　　Wǒ yǒudiǎnr è.
3. 我再点一份莲花血鸭。　　　　Wǒ zài diǎn yí fèn Liánhuā xuèyā.

Warm-up
热身　Rèshēn

读一读下面的菜名，查一查哪些是江西菜？

Read the names of the dishes below and find out which ones are Jiangxi dishes.

Hóngshāoròu
红烧肉

Tángcùyú
糖醋鱼

Sānbēijī
三杯鸡

Liánhuā xuèyā
莲花　血鸭

第一课 你吃过江西菜吗?
LESSON 1 Have you ever had Jiangxi cuisine?

Kèjiā niàngdòufu
客家 酿豆腐

Dāngguī dùnjī
当归 炖鸡

Texts
课文 kèwén

Měinà: Héxī, nǐ è ma? Wǒ yǒudiǎnr è.
美娜:荷西,你饿吗?我有点儿饿。

Héxī: Wǒ yě yǒudiǎnr è.
荷西:我也有点儿饿。

Měinà: Nǐ chīguo Jiāngxī cài ma?
美娜:你吃过江西菜吗?

Héxī: Wǒ tīngshuōguo, dànshì méi chīguo. Nǐ ne?
荷西:我听说过,但是没吃过。你呢?

Měinà: Wǒ chīguo, Jiāngxī cài hěn hǎochī, dànshì hěn là. Nǐ xíguàn chīlà ma?
美娜:我吃过,江西菜很好吃,但是很辣。你习惯吃辣吗?

Héxī: Hái kěyǐ.
荷西:还可以。

Měinà: Wǒ zhīdào yì jiā fànguǎn, nàli de Jiāngxī cài hěn yǒu tèsè. Xià kè hòu wǒmen yìqǐ qù ba.
美娜:我知道一家饭馆,那里的江西菜很有特色。下课后我们一起去吧。

Héxī: Lí xuéxiào yuǎn ma?
荷西:离学校远吗?

Měinà: Bù yuǎn, zǒulù huòzhě qí zìxíngchē qù dōu kěyǐ.
美娜:不远,走路或者骑自行车去都可以。

Héxī: Wǒmen qí zìxíngchē ba.
荷西:我们骑自行车吧。

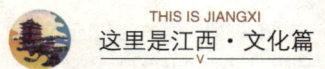

English Version

Mena: Jose, are you hungry? I'm a little hungry.

Jose: I'm a little hungry, too.

Mena: Have you ever had Jiangxi cuisine?

Jose: I've heard of it, but I haven't tried. What about you?

Mena: I have had it. Jiangxi cuisine is delicious but very spicy. Are you accustomed to eating spicy?

Jose: Yes, I can eat spicy food.

Mena: I know a restaurant that serves Jiangxi specialty dish. Let's go there together after class.

Jose: Is it far from our universities?

Mena: Not far. We can walk or cycle there.

Jose: Let's go by bike.

生词   New Words

1. 饿	è	adj.	be hungry
2. 有点儿	yǒudiǎnr	adv.	a bit, a little, slightly
3. 菜	cài	n.	❶dish, cuisine; ❷vegetable
4. 听说	tīngshuō	v.	to hear of
5. 过	guo	part.	used after a verb to indicate the completion of an action
6. 但是	dànshì	conj.	but
7. 习惯	xíguàn	v.&n.	❶to be accustomed to; ❷habit

8. 饭馆	fànguǎn	n.	restaurant
9. 特色	tèsè	n.	salient feature
10. 走路	zǒulù	v.	to walk
11. 或者	huòzhě	conj.	or
12. 自行车	zìxíngchē	n.	bicycle

Texts 课文 kèwén

服务员：欢迎光临，您几位？
Fúwùyuán: Huānyíng guānglín, nín jǐ wèi?

荷西：两位。
Héxī: Liǎng wèi.

服务员：里边请。这是菜单，您可以用手机扫码点餐。
Fúwùyuán: Lǐbian qǐng. Zhè shì càidān, nín kěyǐ yòng shǒujī sǎomǎ diǎn cān.

美娜：你们店有什么特色菜？
Měinà: Nǐmen diàn yǒu shénme tèsè cài?

服务员：我们店的特色菜有三杯鸡、莲花血鸭和客家酿豆腐。
Fúwùyuán: Wǒmen diàn de tèsè cài yǒu Sānbēijī, Liánhuā xuèyā hé Kèjiā niàngdòufu.

美娜：好，我点一份三杯鸡。
Měinà: Hǎo, wǒ diǎn yí fèn Sānbēijī.

荷西：再要一份莲花血鸭。
Héxī: zài yào yí fèn Liánhuā xuèyā.

服务员：这道菜有点儿辣。
Fúwùyuán: Zhè dào cài yǒudiǎnr là.

荷西：没关系。再来两碗米饭，两杯果汁，先点
Héxī: Méi guānxi. Zài lái liǎng wǎn mǐfàn, liǎng bēi guǒzhī, xiān diǎn

zhèxiē ba.
这些 吧。

Fúwùyuán: Hǎo de, qǐng shāo děng !
服务员：好 的，请 稍 等！

Héxī: Xièxie !
荷西：谢谢！

English Version

Waiter: Welcome! Table of how many?

Jose: Two.

Waiter: This way, please. Here is the menu. You can order food by scanning this code with your cell phone.

Mena: Okay, what specialty dishes do you have ?

Waiter: Our specialty dishes include Stewed Chicken with Three Cups of Sauce, Lianhua Braised Duck and Hakka Meat-Stuffed Tofu.

Mena: Okay, I'll have Stewed Chicken with Three Cups of Sauce.

Jose: And I'd like Lianhua Braised Duck.

Waiter: Lianhua Braised Duck would be a little bit spicy.

Mena: That's okay. Also, we'll get two bowls of rice and two glasses of juice. Just these first, please.

Waiter: Okay, please wait a moment.

Jose: Thank you!

生词 *New Words*

1. 位	wèi	m.	a respectful measure word for people
2. 里边	lǐ bian	n.	inside

3. 菜单	càidān	n.	menu	
4. 扫	sǎo	v.	to scan	
5. 点	diǎn	v.	to select from many things	
6. 餐	cān	n.	meal, food	
7. 份	fèn	m.	a set of	
8. 碗	wǎn	m.&n.	❶a bowl of; ❷bowl	
9. 杯	bēi	m.&n.	❶a cup of; ❷cup	
10. 果汁	guǒzhī	n.	fruit juice	

Proper Noun
专有名词　Zhuānyǒu míngcí

三杯鸡	Sānbēijī	Stewed Chicken with Three Cups of Sauce
莲花血鸭	Liánhuā xuèyā	Lianhua Braised Duck
客家酿豆腐	Kèjiā niàngdòufu	Hakka Meat-Stuffed Tofu

Grammar
语法　Yǔfǎ

1. 动态助词"过"　The Aspect Particle "过"

　　动词后加上动态助词"过",一般用来描述过去的经历,这些动作行为没有持续到现在。

　　A verb followed by the aspect particle "过" usually indicates a past experience or action that has not lasted to the present.

（1）我吃过江西菜。

（2）我没去过那个饭馆。

（3）你看过这本书吗？

2. 程度副词"有点儿"　The Adverbial Modifier "有点儿"

"有点儿"用在形容词或者动词前面，表示程度不高，一般用于不满意的事情。

"有点儿" comes before an adjective or a verb. It indicates a slight degree; it is usually used for something dissatisfied.

（1）我有点儿饿。

（2）今天天气有点儿冷。

（3）我有点儿不习惯。

1. 根据课文回答问题　Answer the questions according to the texts

（1）荷西吃过江西菜吗？美娜呢？

（2）美娜觉得江西菜怎么样？

（3）他们可以怎么去饭馆？

（4）这家饭馆有哪些特色菜？

（5）他们点了什么？

2. 选词填空　Choose the appropriate words to fill in the blanks

特色　　饿　　或者　　点餐　　习惯

（1）我＿＿＿＿吃辣。

（2）这家店的菜很有_____。

（3）我没吃早饭，现在有点儿_____。

（4）现在点菜不用菜单，可以手机扫码_____。

（5）我们可以走路_____骑自行车去那里。

3. 把助词"过"放在合适的位置上　Put the auxiliary word "过" in the proper place

（1）我__A__去__B__北京__C__。

（2）我__A__没__B__吃__C__三杯鸡__D__。

（3）荷西__A__和她__B__一起吃__C__饭__D__。

（4）你__A__去__B__三清山__C__没有__D__？

4. 组词成句　Make up sentences with the given words

（1）辣　　江西菜　　有点儿

_____

（2）现在　　冷　　有点儿

_____

（3）吃　明天　去　再　我　一次　江西菜

_____

（4）一次　吗　可以　再　去　我

_____

（5）习惯　江西菜　吃　吗　你

_____

5. 交际练习　Communication task

假设你和朋友一起去饭馆吃饭，尝试用中文点餐。（Suppose you go to a restaurant with your friends, and you will try to order food in Chinese.）

Cultural Tip
文化贴士　Wénhuà tiēshì

茶香酒醇，鱼米之乡——饮食江西

江西物产丰富，自古就被誉为"江南鱼米之乡"，以自己独有的物产和烹饪方式在中华饮食文化中创造了色重味浓、富有特色的菜系——赣菜。

江西地处南北交通干道之上，饮食兼具南北特色。南来北往的客商们为江西带来了全国各地的饮食，故江西菜兼有蜀、湘、鄂、皖、浙、粤等风味，并在多种风味的基础上形成了自己的特色。例如名菜客家酿豆腐，实际源于北方饺子，因南方没有小麦，客家人用油豆腐代替面皮，形成了独具特色的酿豆腐。

江西人无辣不欢，嗜辣程度不亚于湖南人、四川人。在赣西地区，连炒白菜都要加入大量辣椒，所以人们常以"不怕辣"来概括江西的饮食习惯。除了咸辣以外，不少江西菜以甜和鲜为特色，赣中北部的红烧肉、糖醋鱼等，味道甘甜；赣南、赣东的鱼丸、活鲤鱼等，则以鲜香著称。

此外，江西饮食也很注重养生，药膳是江西饮食的一大特色。药膳发源于"药都"樟树，后传至全省各地。银耳莲子汤、当归炖鸡、天麻炖鸭等菜色，既芳香可口，又有防病养生的功效。

Eating in Jiangxi, a land of fish and rice, home to tea and wine

Jiangxi has been known as the "hometown of fish and rice in the south of China" since ancient times, and has created its own unique taste, Gan cuisine, with the colourful, rich and characteristic in Chinese food culture.

Jiangxi is located on the main north-south transport route, so its food has both northern and southern characteristics. Traders from the north and south brought food culture from all over the country to Jiangxi. Therefore, Jiangxi cuisine is a mixture of Shu, Xiang, E, Wan, Zhe and Yue flavours, and has developed its own characteristics. For example, the famous Hakka stuffed tofu, which actually is originated from dumplings from the north. However, because wheat was not available in the south, Hakka people used oiled tofu instead of dough, resulting in the unique stuffed tofu.

No food without spicy flavour can pleased Jiangxi people and their fond for spicy taste is not less than people of Hunan and Sichuan. In the western Jiangxi, even stir-fried cabbage is made with a large amount of chillies. Therefore, so people often use the term "not afraid of spice" to sum up the eating habits of

Jiangxi people. Apart from salty and spicy, many Jiangxi dishes are sweet and fresh, such as braised pork and sweet and sour fish from northern central Jiangxi, while fish balls and live carp from southern and eastern Jiangxi are known for their freshness.

In addition, Jiangxi cuisine is also very concerned with health, and medicinal food is one of the main features of it. The medicinal cuisine originated in Zhangshu, the "capital of medicine", and has then spread throughout the province. Silver fungus and lotus seed soup, chicken stewed with angelica and duck stewed with asparagus are not only aromatic and tasty, but also have the effect of preventing illness and maintaining health.

第二课　我一次景德镇都没去过
LESSON 2　I have never been to Jingdezhen City

- 知识目标：掌握"一……也/都＋不/没……"以及结果补语"好"的用法
- 能力目标：能够用汉语表达过往经历
- 文化目标：了解江西景德镇以及瓷器文化

第二课　我一次景德镇都没去过

Key Sentences
重点句　Zhòngdiǎn jù

1. 我一次景德镇都没去过。　　Wǒ yí cì Jǐngdézhèn dōu méi qùguo.
2. 这是青花瓷吧?　　　　　　Zhè shì Qīnghuācí ba?
3. 花瓶做好了。　　　　　　　Huāpíng zuò hǎo le.

Warm-up
热身　Rèshēn

说一说你身边有哪些东西是瓷器?　Talk about the porcelain in your daily life.

wǎn
碗

pánzi
盘子

huāpíng
花瓶

chájù
茶具

sháozi
勺子

bēizi
杯子

Texts 课文 kèwén

荷西：Héxī: Pí'āi'ěr, nǐ de chábēi zhēn piàoliang, shì Qīnghuācí ba?
皮埃尔，你的茶杯真漂亮，是青花瓷吧？

皮埃尔：Pí'āi'ěr: Shì de, zhè shì wǒ zài diànli mǎi de chájù, shì Jǐngdézhèn de.
是的，这是我在店里买的茶具，是景德镇的。

美娜：Měinà: Tīngshuō Jǐngdézhèn shì Zhōngguó de cídū.
听说景德镇是中国的瓷都。

江南：Jiāng Nán: Shì de, Jǐngdézhèn yǒu Yùyáochǎng, zhuānmén gěi huángdì zuò cíqì.
是的，景德镇有御窑厂，专门给皇帝做瓷器。

美娜：Měinà: Zhēn yǒu yìsi. Wǒ xiǎng qù Jǐngdézhèn wán yi wánr, wǒ yí cì Jǐngdézhèn dōu méi qùguo.
真有意思。我想去景德镇玩一玩儿，我一次景德镇都没去过。

皮埃尔：Pí'āi'ěr: Wǒ yě shì. Kuài fàngjià le, wǒmen yìqǐ qù ba.
我也是。快放假了，我们一起去吧。

美娜：Měinà: Hǎo, wǒmen xiān mǎi gāotiě piào ba.
好，我们先买高铁票吧。

荷西：Héxī: Kěyǐ zài shǒujī shang mǎi piào. Wǒ jiāo nǐmen ba.
可以在手机上买票。我教你们吧。

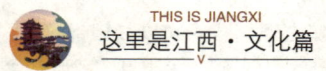

English Version

Jose: Pierre, your teacup is so beautiful. Is it blue and white porcelain?

Pierre: Yes, I bought this tea set in a specialty shop. It's from Jingdezhen.

Mena: I heard that Jingdezhen is the porcelain capital in China.

Jiang Nan: Yes, there is an Imperial Kiln Factory in Jingdezhen, which produced porcelain just for emperors.

Mina: That's interesting. I want to go to Jingdezhen. I have never been to Jingdezhen.

Pierre: Me too. The vacation's coming. Let's go there together.

Mena: Okay, Let's buy high-speed rail tickets first.

Jose: We can buy tickets on cell phone. I'll show you.

生词 New Words

1. 茶杯	chábēi	n.	teacup
2. 瓷器	cíqì	n.	porcelain
3. 以前	yǐqián	adv.	before; previous
4. 专门	zhuānmén	adj.&adv.	❶special; specialized; ❷specially
5. 皇帝	huángdì	n.	emperor
6. 做	zuò	v.	to make; to produce
7. 放假	fàng jià	v.	to have a holiday or vacation
8. 教	jiāo	v.	to teach

第二课　我一次景德镇都没去过
LESSON 2 I have never been to Jingdezhen City

Texts
课文　kèwén

B

美娜：看，那里有人在做瓷器。

皮埃尔：我们也试试吧，我一次瓷器都没做过。

工作人员：您好！请问你们要做瓷器吗？

江南：是的。

工作人员：可以先看看，那边师傅在做瓷器。

荷西：哇！转一会儿就做好了。

工作人员：这叫拉坯。要试试吗？

皮埃尔：好啊。我想做一个花瓶，可以吗？

师傅：可以的，很简单，我教你。

皮埃尔：花瓶做好了，你们觉得怎么样？

美娜：真好看，我也想试试。做好以后可以带走吗？

工作人员：可以的。我们会帮您包好。

English Version

Mena: Look, someone is making porcelain there.

Pierre: Let's try that too. I haven't made porcelain once.

Staff: Hello! Do you want to make porcelain?

Jiang Nan: Yes.

Staff: You can have a look first. The master over there is making porcelain.

Jose: Wow! It gets ready in a few minutes.

Staff: Look, it is called "throwing", means working with the clay on a potter's wheel. Do you want to try?

Pierre: Sure. I want to make a vase, may I?

master: Yes, it's very simple. I'll teach you.

Pierre: The vase is done. Do you like it?

Mena: That's really beautiful. I want to try it, too. Can we bring the porcelain home when it's finished?

Staff: Yes. We will wrap those up for you.

生词 New Words

1. 试   shì   v.   to try
2. 师傅 shīfu n.   master worker (a qualified worker as distinct from an apprentice)
3. 哇   wā   int. wow
4. 转   zhuàn v.   to turn; to revolve

5. 简单	jiǎndān	adj.	easy; simple
6. 好看	hǎokàn	adj.	beautiful
7. 以后	yǐhòu	n.	later
8. 带	dài	v.	to carry; to take; to bring
9. 包	bāo	v.	to wrap up

Proper Noun
专有名词　Zhuānyǒu míngcí

御窑厂	Yùyáochǎng	Imperial Kiln Factory

Grammar
语法　Yǔfǎ

1. 结果补语"好"　The Complement of Result "好"

用在动词的后边，如"做好""吃好"，表示动作完成，并让人满意。

The complement of result "好" follows a verb, as in "做好" and "吃好" to indicate that the action is satisfactorily completed.

（1）花瓶做好了。

（2）我买好票了。

（3）我已经计划好去景德镇玩一玩了。

2. "一……也/都+不/没……"表示否定　The Negative Structure "一……也/都+不/没……"

用"一+量词+（名词）+也/都+不/没+V"表示完全否定。

"一+Measure Word+（Noun）+也/都+不/没+V" indicates complete negation.

（1）我一次景德镇也没去过。

（2）教室里一个人也没有。

（3）她一件新衣服都没买过。

Exercise 练习　Liànxí

1. 根据课文回答问题　Answer the questions according to the texts

（1）皮埃尔的茶杯是在哪儿买的？

（2）美娜去过景德镇吗？

（3）他们是怎么买火车票的？

（4）皮埃尔做了什么瓷器？

（5）谁教皮埃尔和美娜做瓷器的？

2. 选词填空　Choose the appropriate words to fill in the blanks

瓷器　　放假　　师傅　　简单

（1）做_____一点儿也不难。

（2）快_____了，我打算去景德镇玩一玩。

（3）_____正在做瓷器。

（4）这次考试很_____，我都会。

3. 请用"一……也/都+不/没……"回答下面的问题　Please use "一……也/都+不/没……" to answer questions

（1）你的钱包（wallet）里有钱吗？

（2）他买东西了吗？

（3）教室里有人吗？

4. 请把"好"放在合适的位置上　Please put "好" in the proper place

（1）去南昌的__A__高铁票__B__你买__C__了__D__吗？

（2）昨天__A__的作业（homework）__B__你做__C__了__D__吗？

（3）我__A__买__B__了送给妈妈__C__的__D__礼物（gift）。

（4）我__A__已经__B__做__C__了一个__D__花瓶。

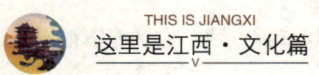

5. 交际练习　Communication task

上网查一查景德镇的资料，在课堂上进行分享。

Look up the information about Jingdezhen on the Internet, and share it with the class.

丝路上的白色金子——景德镇瓷器

景德镇坐落于江西东北部的群山中，是世界陶瓷历史上最负盛名的城市之一。明代时，景德镇成立了御窑厂，专为皇家烧制瓷器。

沿着"陆上丝绸之路"和"海上丝绸之路"，景德镇瓷器曾大量出口国外。

沿古代丝绸之路的陆路，景德镇瓷器被运往中亚细亚及波斯等地，沿海路则被运往波斯湾及地中海各国。

随着海上"丝绸之路"越来越繁忙，景德镇瓷器大量外销。16、17世纪，景德镇瓷器大规模进入欧洲市场。当时，以景德镇瓷器为代表的中国瓷器被誉为"白色金子"，在欧洲风靡一时。在当时的欧洲，穿中国绸、喝中国茶、用中国瓷是上流社会的象征。

瓷器既是商品，也是东方文化的符号。通过瓷器，世界认识了东方，认识了中国。各种文化在瓷器上碰撞、交融，最终展开了一场东西文明经久不息的对话。以瓷为媒介，中华文化发挥出辐射最广、影响最大的效应。

White gold on the Silk Road – Jingdezhen porcelain

Nestled in the mountains of north-eastern Jiangxi, Jingdezhen is one of the most prestigious cities in the history of world ceramics. During the Ming Dynasty, the Imperial Kiln Factory was established in Jingdezhen to make porcelain for the royal family.

Along the "Land Silk Road" and "Sea Silk Road", Jingdezhen porcelain was exported in large quantities to foreign countries. Along the ancient Silk Road by land, Jingdezhen porcelain was shipped to Central Asia and Persia; it also reached the Persian Gulf and Mediterranean countries by sea.

As the sea "Silk Road" became busier and busier, Jingdezhen porcelain was exported in large quantities. In 16, 17 centuries, Jingdezhen porcelain into the European market on a large scale. At that time, Jingdezhen porcelain as the representative of the Chinese porcelain was sweeping the Europe, and won praise

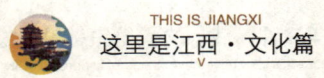

as the "white gold". European high society began to wear Chinese silk, drinking Chinese tea and using Chinese porcelain.

Porcelain was not only a commodity but also a symbol of Eastern culture. Through porcelain, the world got to know the East and China. Various cultures collided and mingled on porcelain, eventually launching an enduring dialogue between eastern and western civilisations. With porcelain as a medium, Chinese culture has played the most radiant and influential effect.

第三课　滕王阁有多高？
LESSON 3 How tall is the Tengwang Pavilion?

- 知识目标：了解并掌握"是……的"、趋向补语和疑问代词"多"的用法
- 能力目标：能够用汉语进行邀约
- 文化目标：了解滕王阁

第三课 滕王阁有多高？

Key Sentences
重点句 Zhòngdiǎn jù

1. 你是什么时候去的？   Nǐ shì shénme shíhou qù de ?
2. 我们上去看看吧。   Wǒmen shàng qù kànkan ba.
3. 你站过来一点儿。   Nǐ zhàn guòlai yìdiǎnr.

Warm-up
热身 Rèshēn

说一说，你知道哪些中国的著名建筑？ Talk about the famous buildings you know in China.

TiānTán
天 坛

Dì Tán
地 坛

Dàyàn Tǎ
大 雁 塔

Huánghè Tóu
黄 鹤 楼

第三课　滕王阁有多高？
LESSON 3 How tall is the Tengwang Pavilion?

Yuèyáng Lóu
岳阳楼

Téngwáng Gé
腾王阁

Texts
课文　kèwén

Pí'āi'ěr：　Jiāng Nán, zhōumò nǐ dǎsuan zuò shénme?
皮埃尔：　江南，周末你打算做什么？

Jiāng Nán：Wǒ hái méi xiǎng hǎo, nǐ ne?
江　南：我还没想好，你呢？

Pí'āi'ěr：　Lái Nánchāng zhème jiǔ le, wǒ hái méi qùguo Téngwáng Gé.
皮埃尔：　来南昌这么久了，我还没去过腾王阁。
　　　　　Tīngshuō Téngwáng Gé hěn piàoliang, wǒ xiǎng qù kànkan.
　　　　　听说腾王阁很漂亮，我想去看看。

Jiāng Nán：Téngwáng Gé hěn yǒumíng. Nǐ méi qùguo Téngwáng Gé ma?
江　南：腾王阁很有名。你没去过腾王阁吗？

Pí'āi'ěr：　Wǒ méi qùguo.
皮埃尔：　我没去过。

Jiāng Nán：Wǒ qùguo yí cì.
江　南：我去过一次。

Pí'āi'ěr：　Nǐ shì shénme shíhou qù de?
皮埃尔：　你是什么时候去的？

Jiāng Nán：Xiǎoshíhou qù de. Wǒ xiǎng zài qù yí cì.
江　南：小时候去的。我想再去一次。

Pí'āi'ěr：　Tài hǎo le. Wǒmen yìqǐ qù ba. Zhègè xīngqī liù shàngwǔ
皮埃尔：　太好了。我们一起去吧。这个星期六上午
　　　　　zěnmeyàng?
　　　　　怎么样？

Jiāng Nán：Méi wèntí. Wǒmen jǐ diǎn jiàn?
江　南：没问题。我们几点见？

Pí'āi'ěr: Shàngwǔ jiǔ diǎn zài Téngwáng Gé ménkǒu jiàn, zěnmeyàng?
皮埃尔：上午 九点 在 滕王阁 门口 见，怎么样？

Jiāng Nán: Hǎo de, xīngqī liù jiàn.
江 南：好的，星期 六 见。

Pí'āi'ěr: Xīngqī liù jiàn.
皮埃尔：星期 六 见。

English Version

Pierre: Jiang Nan, what are you going to do on the weekend?

Jiang Nan: I haven't decided yet, and you?

Pierre: I have been in Nanchang for so long. I haven't been to Tengwang Pavilion. It is said that Tengwang Pavilion is very beautiful. I want to go and see it.

Jiang Nan: Tengwang Pavilion is very famous, Haven't you never been there?

Pierre: Not yet.

Jiang Nan: I went there once before.

Pierre: When did you go there?

Jiang Nan: When I was a child. I would like to go there again.

Pierre: Great. Let's go together. What about this Saturday morning?

Jiang Nan: No problem. What time would you like to meet?

Pierre: How about meeting at the entrance of Tengwang Pavilion at 9:00 AM.

Jiang Nan:Okay, see you on Saturday.

Pierre:See you.

第三课 滕王阁有多高?
LESSON 3 How tall is the Tengwang Pavilion?

生词 New Words

1.	周末	zhōumò	n.	weekend
2.	这么	zhème	adv.	so; such
3.	久	jiǔ	adj.	long, long time
4.	有名	yǒumíng	adj.	famous
5.	小时候	xiǎoshíhou	n.	in one's childhood
6.	见	jiàn	v.	to see; to meet
7.	门口	ménkǒu	n.	entrance; gateway

Texts 课文 kèwén

Jiāng Nán: Nǐ hǎo, Pí'āi'ěr!
江 南: 你好,皮埃尔!

Pí'āi'ěr: Nǐ hǎo, Jiāng Nán. Nǐ shì zěnme lái de?
皮埃尔: 你好,江 南。你是怎么来的?

Jiāng Nán: Wǒ shì zuò dìtiě lái de. Nǐ ne?
江 南: 我是坐地铁来的。你呢?

Pí'āi'ěr: Wǒ shì dǎchē lái de. Yǐjīng jiǔ diǎn le, wǒmen jìnqu ba!
皮埃尔: 我是打车来的。已经九点了,我们进去吧!

Jiāng Nán: Téngwáng Gé yìdiǎnr dōu méi biàn, háishì zhème piàoliang.
江 南: 滕王阁 一点儿都没变,还是这么漂亮。

Pí'āi'ěr: Shì a, yòu gāo yòu piàoliang. Téngwáng Gé yǒu duō gāo?
皮埃尔: 是啊,又高又漂亮。 滕王阁 有多高?

Jiāng Nán: Téngwáng Gé gāo wǔshíqī diǎn wǔ mǐ, wǒmen shàngqu kànkan ba.
江 南: 滕王阁 高 57.5 米,我们上去看看吧。

Pí'āi'ěr: Hǎo a. Téngwáng Gé yígòng yǒu jǐ céng?
皮埃尔: 好啊。滕王阁 一共有几层?

Jiāng Nán: Yígòng qī céng. Nàbian yǒu lóutī hé diàntī. Wǒmen zuò
江 南：一共 七层。那边 有 楼梯 和 电梯。我们 坐
diàntī shàngqu, háishi zǒu shàngqu?
电梯 上去，还是 走 上去？

Pí'āi'ěr: Wǒ xiǎng zǒu shàngqu.
皮埃尔：我 想 走 上去。

Jiāng Nán: Hǎo, zǒu ba! Shàngmian kěyǐ kàndào Gànjiāng.
江 南：好，走 吧！ 上面 可以 看到 赣江。

Pí'āi'ěr: Lóushang de fēngjǐng
皮埃尔：楼上 的 风景
hěn měi, wǒmen pāi
很美，我们 拍
zhāng zhàopiàn ba.
张 照片 吧。

Jiāng Nán: Hǎo a, nǐ zhàn
江 南：好啊，你 站
guòlai yìdiǎnr.
过来 一点儿。

English Version

Jiang Nan: Hello, Pierre.

Pierre: Hello, Jiang Nan. How did you get here?

Jiang Nan: I took the subway, and you?

Pierre: I took a taxi. It's already 9:00. Let's get in!

Jiang Nan: Tengwang Pavilion doesn't change at all. It's still so beautiful.

Pierre: Yeah, it's so high and so beautiful. What is the height of Tengwang Pavilion?

Jiang Nan: The height of Tengwang Pavilion is 57.5 meters, let's go up and have a look.

Pierre: Okay, how many floors are there in Tengwang Pavilion?

Jiang Nan: Totally seven floors. There are stairs and elevators over there. Shall we go upstairs by taking elevators or stairs?

Jiang Nan: I want to take the stairs.

Pierre: Okay, let's go.

Jiang Nan: Let's go. We can see the Gan River upstairs.

Pierre: The views from upstairs is so beautiful. Let's take a photo together.

Jiang Nan: Okay, come closer to me.

生词 New Words

1. 打车	dǎchē	v.	to take a taxi
2. 进	jìn	v.	to enter
3. 已经	yǐjīng	adv.	already
4. 变	biàn	v.	to change
5. 米	mǐ	m.	meter
6. 层	céng	m.	floor
7. 楼	lóu	n.	❶building; ❷floor
8. 楼梯	lóutī	n.	stairs
9. 电梯	diàntī	n.	elevator
10. 楼上	lóushang	n.	upstairs
11. 风景	fēngjǐng	n.	scenery, landscape

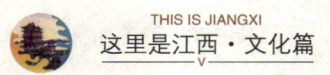

Proper Noun
专有名词 Zhuānyǒu míngcí

| 赣江 | Gànjiāng | Gan River, a branch of the Yangtze River |

Grammar
语法 Yǔfǎ

1. "是……的"句型 The Sentence Structure "是……的"

"是……的"句型强调已经发生动作的时间、地点、方式等。肯定句和疑问句中"是"字可以省略，否定句中不能省略。

The structure "是……的" can be used to emphasize the time, location, and the manner when the action occurred. "是" can be omitted in positive and interrogative sentences, but cannot be omitted in negative sentences.

（1）你是怎么来的？

（2）他们是上午来的。

（3）我们不是在滕王阁认识的。

2. 趋向补语 Complements of Direction

①简单趋向补语 Simple Complements of Direction

"V+来/去"是简单趋向补语，表示动作的方向。"来"表示该动作朝着说话人的方向，"去"表示该动作与说话人的方向背离。常用的七个动词为"上、下、进、出、回、过、起"。

"V+来/去" severs as the simple complements of direction, indicating the direction of an action. "来" indicates the direction towards the speaker, while "去"

indicates the direction is away from the speaker. The 7 most frequently used verbs are "上、下、进、出、回、过、起".

	上	下	进	出	回	过	起
来	上来	下来	进来	出来	回来	过来	起来
去	上去	下去	进去	出去	回去	过去	

其中"起"只与"来"连用。如果宾语是处所，宾语放在"来/去"的前边；如果宾语是事物名词，既可放在"来/去"的前边，也可放在"来/去"的后边。

"起" is only used with "来". If the object is a place, it should be put before "来/去"; if the object is a thing, it can be put before or after "来/去".

（1）我们进去吧。

（2）你早上几点过来？

（3）我们进去吧。

（4）我后天回来。

②复合趋向补语　Compound Complements of Direction

"上、下、进、出、回、过、起"这七个趋向动词与"来/去"连用，作为别的动词的补语，表示动作的方向，描述相应的动作。宾语是处所时，要放在"来/去"之前；宾语是人或者物时，既可放在"来/去"之前，也可放在"来/去"之后。

The seven directional verbs "上、下、进、出、回、过、起" combined with "来/去", which can be used after another verb as its complement. And it indicates the direction of the action and describes the action. If the object is a place, it should be put before "来/去"; if the object is a person or a thing, it can be put before or after "来/去".

（1）我们一起走上去吧。

（2）你站过来一点儿。

（3）书已经带回去了。

（4）从我家走过来要半个小时。

（5）他买回来一个杯子。

3. 疑问代词"多" The Interrogative Pronoun "多"

疑问代词"多"用在形容词前面，用于对事物的程度提问。例如：

The interrogative pronoun "多" is used before an adjective, asking about the degree of something.

（1）滕王阁有多高？

（2）你今年多大？

（3）学校离火车站有多远？

1. 根据课文回答问题 Answer the questions according to the texts

（1）滕王阁在哪儿？

（2）滕王阁有多高？

（3）滕王阁有名吗？

（4）站在滕王阁上能看到什么？

（5）滕王阁上的风景怎么样？

2. 选择适当的词语填空 Choose the appropriate words to fill in the blanks

小时候　　见面　　打车　　电梯　　进

（1）我们坐_____上去吧。

（2）明天早上8点我跟朋友_____。

（3）他_____去过滕王阁。

（4）皮埃尔是_____来学校的。

（5）老师走_____教室来。

3. 根据所给的词回答问题　Answer the question with the given words

（1）你们是怎么来的？

_____（打车）

（2）老师怎么上去的？

_____（走）

（3）他多高？

_____（米）

（4）他们是什么时候认识的？

_____（小时候）

（5）他买回来什么了？

_____（一盒鸡蛋）

4. 组词成句　Make up sentences with the given words

（1）走路　　来　　的　　他　　是

_____

（2）买　　他　　书　　回　　一本　　来

_____

（3）今年　　多　　老师　　大

_____

（4）走　她　家　回　去

_____

（5）见面的　在　滕王阁　他们　门口　是

_____

5. 交际练习　Communication task

用汉语介绍一个你去过的旅游景点。

Please introduce a scenic spot that you have visited before in Chinese.

_____
_____
_____
_____
_____
_____
_____
_____

Cultural Tip
文化贴士　Wénhuà tiēshì

千年名楼——滕王阁

说起南昌，人们就会想起滕王阁。来到南昌，一定要游览滕王阁。滕王阁位于赣江东岸，始建于唐永徽四年（公元653年），由滕王李元婴修建，因唐代诗人王勃所作《滕王阁序》而闻名于世。滕王阁与湖南岳阳楼、湖北武汉黄鹤楼并称"江南三大名楼"。唐代文学家韩愈在唐元和十五年（公元820年）所写《新修滕王阁记》中，曾赞美道："愈少时，则闻江南多临观之美，而滕王阁独为第一，有瑰伟绝特之称。"

滕王阁主体建筑高57.5米，建筑面积13000平方米；其下部为12米高台座，分为两级。台座以上的主阁取"明三暗七"格式，即从外面看是三层带回廊建筑，而内部却有七层[①]。

面对雄伟的滕王阁，王勃写诗，韩愈撰记，自此开创了"诗文传阁"的先河，吸引了历代文人来到滕王阁登临抒怀。千百年来，文人墨客登阁抒怀相习成风，以挥毫题诗作赋为荣。他们指点江山，激扬文字，抒发思古之情、爱国之心。名景、名人、名作，令江南名楼滕王阁享千秋不朽之誉。

Tengwang Pavilion, a famous building for thousands of years

When people think of Nanchang, they think of Tengwang Pavilion; when they come to Nanchang, they must visit Tengwang Pavilion. Located on the east bank of the Gan River, Tengwang Pavilion was built in the fourth year of the Tang Dynasty's Yong Hui period（653 AD）by Li Yuanying, the King of Teng, and is famous for the preface to *Tengwang Pavilion* written by the Tang poet Wang Bo. Tengwang Pavilion is one of the three most famous buildings in Jiangnan, together with Yueyanglou in Hunan and Huanghelou in Wuhan, Hubei. Han Yu, a Tang Dynasty writer, wrote *The New Repair of Tengwang Pavilion* in the 15th year of the Tang Dynasty's Yuan He period（820 AD）, and praised it: "When I was young,

---

① 数据来自南昌滕王阁景区官方网。

I heard that there were many beautiful places in Jiangnan, but Tengwang Pavilion was the first, with a magnificent and unique name."

The main building of the Tengwang Pavilion is 57.5 metres high, with a construction area of 13,000 square metres; its lower part is a 12-metre high pedestal, divided into two levels. The main pavilion above the pedestal is in the "bright three dark seven" format, i.e. from the outside it is a three-storey building with a corridor, while inside it has seven storeys.

In the face of the majestic Tengwang Pavilion, Wang Bo wrote poetry and Han Yu wrote prose, thus creating a precedent of "literature and architecture" and attracting literati from all generations to Tengwang Pavilion to express their feelings. For thousands of years, it has been the custom of the literati to express their sentiments in the Pavilion, taking pride in inscribing their poems and composing fictions. They pointed to the mountains and rivers, and expressed their feelings of antiquity and patriotism. The famous scenery, celebrities and masterpieces have made the Tengwang Pavilion, a famous building in Jiangnan, enjoy an immortal reputation for thousands of years.

第四课　文港毛笔的历史真悠久

LESSON 4 The history of Wengang writing brush is really long

- 知识目标：掌握"多"表示概数和连词"那"的用法
- 能力目标：学会用汉语谈论某件事物的历史
- 文化目标：了解江西文港毛笔

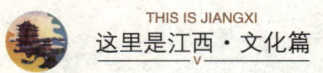

第四课　文港毛笔的历史真悠久

Key Sentences
重点句　Zhòngdiǎn jù

1. 文港毛笔历史真悠久。　　　Wéngǎng máobǐ lìshǐ zhēn yōujiǔ.
2. 文港毛笔有一千七百　　　　Wéngǎng máobǐ yǒu yìqiān qībǎi
   多年的历史。　　　　　　　duō nián de lìshǐ.
3. 那您一定很厉害了。　　　　Nà nín yídìng hěn lìhai le.

Warm-up
热身　Rèshēn

你了解中国书法和绘画吗？

Do you know Chinese calligraphy and painting?

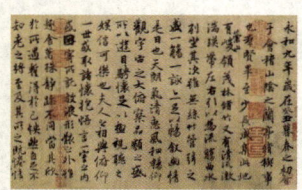

shūfǎ
书法

guóhuà
国画

máobǐ
毛笔

mò
墨

zhǐ
纸

yàn
砚

Texts 课文 kèwén

Wáng Yuè: Dàjiā hǎo, zhèli shì Wéngǎng. Zhèli de máobǐ
王 月：大家 好，这里 是 文港。这里 的 毛笔

hěn yǒumíng.
很 有名。

Héxī: Wáng lǎoshī, wǒ zhīdào Zhōngguó de shūfǎ, dànshì duì máobǐ
荷西：王 老师，我 知道 中国 的 书法，但是 对 毛笔

bú tài liǎojiě.
不太 了解。

Wáng Yuè: Máobǐ shì shūfǎ hé huàhua de gōngjù. Zhōngguó rén hěn zǎo jiù
王 月：毛笔 是 书法 和 画画 的 工具。中国 人 很 早 就

kāishǐ zuò máobǐ le. Wéngǎng de máobǐ yǒu yìqiān qībǎi
开始 做 毛笔 了。文港 的 毛笔 有 一千 七百

duō nián de lìshǐ.
多 年 的 历史。

Měinà: Wā! Wéngǎng máobǐ lìshǐ zhēn yōujiǔ.
美娜：哇！ 文港 毛笔 历史 真 悠久。

Pí'āi'ěr: Wáng lǎoshī, nín kàn, nà wèi shīfu shì zài zuò máobǐ ma?
皮埃尔：王 老师，您 看，那 位 师傅 是 在 做 毛笔 吗？

Wáng Yuè: Shì de. Wǒmen qù nàr cānguān yíxià ba.
王 月：是 的。我们 去 那儿 参观 一下 吧。

Héxī: Shīfu nín hǎo, qǐng wèn zuò máobǐ nán ma?
荷西：师傅 您 好，请 问 做 毛笔 难 吗？

Shīfu: Zuò máobǐ bù nán, dànshì xūyào yǒu nàixīn.
师傅：做 毛笔 不 难，但是 需要 有 耐心。

Pí'āi'ěr: Nín zuò máobǐ duōshao nián le?
皮埃尔：您 做 毛笔 多少 年 了？

Shīfu: Wǒ shíqī suì xuéxí zuò máobǐ, dào xiànzài yǐjīng zuò le
师傅：我 十七 岁 学习 做 毛笔，到 现在 已经 做 了
wǔshí duō nián le.
五十 多 年 了。

Pí'āi'ěr: Nà nín yídìng hěn lìhai le, wǒ kěyǐ gěi nín lù yí gè
皮埃尔：那 您 一定 很 厉害 了，我 可以 给 您 录 一 个
shìpín ma?
视频 吗？

Shīfu: Dāngrán kěyǐ.
师傅：当然 可以。

English Version

Wang Yue: Hello, everyone, here is Wengang. It is famous for the writing brush.

Jose: Ms. Wang, I know Chinese calligraphy, but I don't know much about writing brush.

Wang Yue: Writing brush is a tool for calligraphy and Chinese painting. Chinese people began to make writing brush long time ago. Wengang writing brush has a history of more than one thousand seven hundred years.

Mena: Wow! Wengang writing brush has a long history.

Pierre: Ms. Wang, is that master worker making writing brushes?

Wang Yue: Yes. Let's go there and have a look.

Jose: Hello, master, is it difficult to make writing brush?

Master: It's not difficult to make writing brush, but it needs patience.

第四课　文港毛笔的历史真悠久
LESSON 4 The history of Wengang writing brush is really long

Pierre: How many years have you been making writing brushes?
Master: I learned to make writing brush at the age of seventeen, and have been doing it for more than fifty years till now.
Pierre: That's very impressive. Can I record a video for you?
Master: Of course.

生词　*New Words*

1. 毛笔	máobǐ	n.	writing brush
2. 书法	shūfǎ	n.	calligraphy
3. 工具	gōngjù	n.	tool
4. 画	huà	v.&n.	to paint; painting
5. 千	qiān	m.	thousand
6. 历史	lìshǐ	n.	history
7. 悠久	yōujiǔ	adj.	Long time
8. 写	xiě	v.	to write
9. 参观	cānguān	v.	to visit
10. 耐心	nàixīn	n.	patience
11. 年	nián	n.	year
12. 一定	yídìng	adv.	definitely
13. 厉害	lìhai	adj	terrific; extraordinary
14. 录	lù	v.	to record
15. 视频	shìpín	n.	video

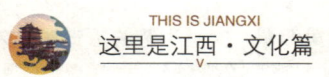

Texts
课文 kèwén

荷西： 这儿的毛笔真多！我们去买毛笔吧。
Héxī: Zhèr de máobǐ zhēn duō! Wǒmen qù mǎi máobǐ ba.

皮埃尔： 好啊，那我们快去吧。
Pí'āi'ěr: Hǎo a, nà wǒmen kuài qù ba.

售货员： 你们好，你们想买什么？
Shòuhuòyuán: Nǐmen hǎo, nǐmen xiǎng mǎi shénme?

皮埃尔： 我想买毛笔。
Pí'āi'ěr: Wǒ xiǎng mǎi máobǐ.

售货员： 我们有各式各样的毛笔，有画画儿用的，还有写书法用的。您需要哪种？
Shòuhuòyuán: Wǒmen yǒu gèshìgèyàng de máobǐ, yǒu huà huàr yòng de, hái yǒu xiě shūfǎ yòng de. Nín xūyào nǎ zhǒng?

皮埃尔： 我想学习中国的书法，要写书法的。有墨水吗？再要一瓶墨水。
Pí'āi'ěr: Wǒ xiǎng xuéxí Zhōngguó de shūfǎ, yào xiě shūfǎ de. Yǒu mòshuǐ ma? Zài yào yì píng mòshuǐ.

荷西： 我想学习画中国画，我要画画儿的。
Héxī: Wǒ xiǎng xuéxí huà Zhōngguó huà, wǒ yào huà huàr de.

售货员： 两支毛笔，一瓶墨水。还要什么吗？
Shòuhuòyuán: Liǎng zhī máobǐ, yì píng mòshuǐ. Hái yào shénme ma?

皮埃尔： 还要一盒颜料。
Pí'āi'ěr: Hái yào yì hé yánliào.

售货员： 好的。一共一百五十块钱。扫码支付还是现金支付？
Shòuhuòyuán: Hǎo de. Yígòng yìbǎi wǔshí kuài qián. Sǎo mǎ zhīfù hái shì xiànjīn zhīfù?

LESSON 4　The history of Wengang writing brush is really long

　　　　　　Héxī:　　　Nà sǎo mǎ　zhīfù ba.　Fù wán le.
　　　荷西：　那 扫 码 支付 吧。付 完 了。
　　Shòuhuòyuán: Hǎo de,　gěi nín　xiǎopiào. Huānyíng　xiàcì　guānglín.
　　售货员：好 的，给 您 小票。欢迎 下次 光临。

English Version

Jose: There are so many writing brushes here! Let's go to buy writing brushes.

Pierre: Okay, let's go.

Clerk: Hello, what do you want to buy?

Pierre: I want to buy a writing brush.

Clerk: We have all kinds of writing brushes, for drawing, and for writing calligraphy. What kind do you need?

Pierre: I want to learn Chinese calligraphy and need one brush for writing. Do you have any ink? I also need a bottle of ink.

Jose: I want to learn Chinese painting. I want to use it for drawing.

Clerk: Two brushes, a bottle of ink. Anything else?

Jose: I'll have a box of pigment.

Clerk: Okay. That'll be one hundred and fifty yuan altogether. Code scanning or cash?

Jose: Scan the code to pay. Done.

Clerk: Okay, here is your receipt. Please come again.

生词　New Words

1. 需要　　　xūyào　　　　v.　　　to need

2. 各式各样	gèshìgèyàng	idm.	all kinds of
3. 支	zhī	m.	a measure word used with long, stick-like objects
4. 瓶	píng	m.	bottle
5. 墨水	mòshuǐ	n.	ink
6. 颜料	yánliào	n.	pigment
7. 支付	zhīfù	v.	to pay
8. 现金	xiànjīn	n.	cash
9. 小票	xiǎopiào	n.	receipt

Proper Noun
专有名词 Zhuānyǒu míngcí

文港	Wéngǎng	Wengang Town, a town in Jiangxi

Grammar
语法 Yǔfǎ

1. "多"表示概数　Approximate Numbers Indicated by "多"

用"多"表示概数，"多"用在"十、百、千、万"等整数的后面。

Approximate numbers indicated by "多", "多" follows integers like "十(ten), 百(hundred), 千(thousand), 万(ten thousand)".

（1）我学了五十多天。

（2）这个杯子三百多块钱。

（3）文港毛笔有一千七百多年的历史。

2. 连词"那" The Conjunction "那"

连词"那"放在句首，表示根据上文的语意得出的结果。上文可以是对方的话，也可以是自己提出的问题或假设。

The conjunction "那", often used at the beginning of a sentence, indicates a presumable result from what is entailed in the preceding sentence uttered by oneself or someone else.

（1）A: 听说滕王阁很有名。

　　　B: 那我们去参观一下吧。

（2）A: 大家都来了。

　　　B: 那我们开始吧。

（3）下雨了，那你明天再去吧。

3. "的"字短语 "的" Phrase

"的"放在名词、代词、动词、形容词后构成"的"字短语。"的"字短语相当于名词，主要作主语和宾语。

When the structural particle "的" is put after a noun, a pronoun, a verb or an adjective, it becomes a "的" phrase. The "的" phrase functions as a noun and can be used as the subject or object.

（1）这支毛笔是荷西的。

（2）这是我的，不是你的。

（3）这盒颜料有红的、黄的、黑的。

（4）我去超市买了吃的、喝的、用的。

Exercise 练习 Liànxí

1. 根据课文回答问题　Answer the questions according to the texts

（1）什么是毛笔？

（2）做毛笔难吗？

（3）师傅做了多少年的毛笔？

（4）皮埃尔买毛笔做什么？荷西呢？

（5）他们买了什么？一共多少钱？

2. 组词成句　Make up sentence with the given word

（1）一千七百　　文港毛笔　　多　　历史　　有　　年

_____

（2）那　　我们　　去　　快　　吧

_____

（3）手机　　这个　　块　　钱　　多　　两千

_____

（4）二十　　我　　岁　　多　　了

_____

3. 选词填空　Choose the appropriate words to fill in the blanks

　　　　参观　　耐心　　瓶　　各式各样　　一定

（1）他是一个有_____的人。

（2）我买一_____墨水。

（3）我们去那儿_____一下吧。

（4）这里有_____的毛笔。

（5）那家饭馆的菜_____很好吃吧。

4. 用"……的"完成句子　Complete the sentences with "……的"

（1）这些书都是_____。

（2）这件衣服是_____。

（3）这是_____，那是_____。

（4）我的毛笔是在文港_____。

5. 交际练习　Communication

上网查一查毛笔的资料，在课堂上进行分享。

Look up the information about writing brush on the Internet, and share it with the class.

_____
_____
_____
_____
_____
_____
_____
_____
_____

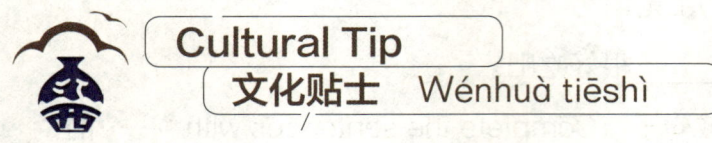

华夏笔都——文港

　　书法是中国文化的代表，笔墨纸砚是书法的基本工具，被称为"文房四宝"。毛笔作为文房四宝之首，在中国有着至少两千多年的历史。江西的文港镇因其高超的制笔工艺，被称为"华夏笔都"、"中国毛笔之乡"。

　　文港镇，坐落在鄱阳湖畔，地处抚河之滨，古属临川，今属进贤。文港制笔的历史可上溯到东汉，已有1700多年历史[①]。文港毛笔素以制作精湛、刚柔相济、书写自如、经久耐用等特点闻名。晋代著名的书法家王羲之在临川时，常使用文港毛笔。初唐才子王勃在其流芳千古的《滕王阁序》中，曾以"光照临川之笔"的佳句，盛赞临川才子敏捷的才思和精妙的书法。文港毛笔也因此增色加辉，更添盛名。

　　明清之际人才辈出，当地以周虎臣为代表的制笔工匠在文港镇及附近的李渡镇等地开设笔庄，形成了江西毛笔产业群。乾隆年间，周虎臣笔庄被地方官员指派为宫廷制作贡笔，其所制的笔得到了乾隆的赞赏，特赐周虎臣笔庄牌匾。晚清时期，中国四家笔庄以其精湛的工艺被称为"四大名笔"，其中两家笔庄的创始人周虎臣、邹紫光都来自文港镇，另一家笔庄的创始人李福寿的祖籍也在李渡镇。

　　坚守传统，代际相传是文港优质毛笔得以传承和发展的关键。文港毛笔经历代艺人千锤百炼，技术日臻完善。2006年，文港毛笔制作技艺被列

---

① 趣闻江西[M].黄明亮,万剑敏,喻峰主编.北京:旅游教育出版社,2006.

入江西省第一批非物质文化遗产名录,并于2021年入选第五批国家级非物质文化遗产名录。

Writing Brush Capital of China – Wen Gang

Calligraphy is a representative of Chinese culture, and the basic tool for calligraphy is the writing brush, ink, paper and ink stone, known as the "Four Treasures of the Writing House". As the first of the four literary treasures, the brush has a history of at least two thousand years in China. The town of Wengang in Jiangxi is known as the "Writing Brush Capital of China" and the "Hometown of Chinese Brushes" due to its superb pen-making techniques.

Located on the shore of Poyang Lake and on the shore of the Fuxiang River, Wengang Town belonged to Linchuan in the past and Jinxian today. The history of making pens in Wengang dates back to the Eastern Han Dynasty, with a history of more than 1700 years. The Wen Gang brush is known for its exquisite production, flexibility, ease of writing and durability. The famous calligrapher Wang Xizhi of the Jin Dynasty often used Wen Gang brushes when he was in Linchuan. Wang Bo, a genius of the early Tang Dynasty, praised the agile talent of Linchuan's talented men and their exquisite calligraphy with the phrase "the light shines on Linchuan's brush" in his "Preface to the Tengwang Pavilion", which has become famous throughout the ages. This is why the Wen Gang brush is so famous.

During the Ming and Qing dynasties, the local brush makers, represented by Zhou Huchen, emerged in large numbers, and opened brush-making villages in Wengang town and the nearby Lidu town, forming the Jiangxi brush industry.

During the Qianlong period, Zhou Huchen was assigned by local officials to make tribute brushes for the court, which was so much appreciated by Qianlong that he gave Zhou Huchen a plaque. During the Republican period of the late Qing Dynasty, four brush-making villages were known as the "Four Famous Brushes" for their exquisite craftsmanship, two of which were founded by Zhou Huchen and Zou Ziguang, both from the town of Wengang, and the founder of another brush-making village, Li Fushou, whose ancestral home was also in the town of Lidu.

The key to the inheritance and development of quality brushes in Wengang is the adherence to tradition and the passing down of brushes from generation to generation. In 2006, the technique was included in the first batch of the Jiangxi intangible cultural heritage list, and in 2021 it was selected for the fifth batch of the national intangible cultural heritage list.

第五课　我一边喝茶一边欣赏庐山美景
LESSON 5　I enjoyed the beautiful scenery of Mount Lushan while drinking tea

- 知识目标：掌握"一边……一边……""因为……所以……"的用法及"再"和"又"的区别
- 能力目标：能够用汉语简单地描述旅行经历
- 文化目标：了解江西的茶文化

第五课 我一边喝茶一边欣赏庐山美景

Key Sentences
重点句　Zhòngdiǎn jù

1. 你怎么又去庐山了？ Nǐ zěnme yòu qù Lúshān le?
2. 我还想再去一次。 Wǒ hái xiǎng zài qù yí cì.
3. 我一边喝茶一边欣赏庐山美景。 Wǒ yìbiān hē chá yìbiān xīnshǎng Lúshān měijǐng.

Warm-up
热身　Rèshēn

你喜欢喝茶吗？你知道江西的哪些茶？

Do you like tea? What type of Chinese tea do you know?

Xīhú Lóngjǐngchá
西湖　龙井茶

Xiūshuǐ Nínghóngchá
修水　宁红茶

Wùyuán Lǜchá
婺源　绿茶

Lúshān Yúnwùchá
庐山　云雾茶

第五课 我一边喝茶一边欣赏庐山美景
LESSON 5　I enjoyed the beautiful scenery of Mount Lushan while drinking tea

Suìchuān Gǒugǔ'nǎochá
遂川 狗牯脑茶

Jǐngdézhèn Fúliángchá
景德镇 浮梁茶

Texts
课文　kèwén

Pí'āi'ěr: Shàng zhōumò nǐ qù nǎr le?
皮埃尔：上 周末 你 去 哪儿 了？

Měinà: Wǒ qù le yí tàng Lúshān.
美娜：我 去 了 一 趟 庐山。

Pí'āi'ěr: Nǐ zěnme yòu qù Lúshān le?
皮埃尔：你 怎么 又 去 庐山 了？

Měinà: Yīnwèi wǒ hěn xǐhuan nàr, suǒyǐ zhè cì wǒ yòu qù le.
美娜：因为 我 很 喜欢 那儿，所以 这 次 我 又 去 了。

Pí'āi'ěr: Zhè cì nǐ qù le nǎxiē dìfang?
皮埃尔：这 次 你 去 了 哪些 地方？

Měinà: Wǒ qù le Sāndié Quán, Wǔlǎo Fēng hé Gǔlǐng Zhèn. Wǒ hái xiǎng
美娜：我 去 了 三叠泉、五老峰 和 牯岭镇。我 还 想
zài qù yí cì.
再 去 一 次。

Pí'āi'ěr: Tīngshuō Jiāngxī yǒu hěn duō hǎo chá, nǐ hēguo ma?
皮埃尔：听说 江西 有 很 多 好 茶，你 喝过 吗？

Měinà: Wǒ hēguo. Lúshān Yúnwùchá fēicháng hǎohē. Wǒ yìbiān hē
美娜：我 喝过。庐山 云雾茶 非常 好喝。我 一边 喝
chá yìbiān xīnshǎng Lúshān měijǐng, hěn shūfu. Lúshān shì gè
茶 一边 欣赏 庐山 美景，很 舒服。庐山 是 个
xiūxián de hǎo dìfang.
休闲 的 好 地方。

Pí'āi'ěr: Yǐhòu yǒu jīhuì de huà, wǒ yě xiǎng qù Lúshān lǚyóu.
皮埃尔：以后 有 机会 的 话，我 也 想 去 庐山 旅游。

English Version

Pierre: Where did you go last weekend?

Mena: I went to Mount Lushan.

Pierre: Why did you go there again?

Mena: Since I love there so much, I went there again this time.

Pierre: Where did you visit this time?

Mena: I went to Sandie Waterfall, Wulao Peak and Kuling Town. I would like to go again.

Pierre: I heard that there are many good teas in Jiangxi province, have you ever tried it?

Mena: I drank it before. The Lushan Yunwu Tea tastes really good. I enjoyed the beautiful scenery of Mount Lushan while drinking tea, it was very relaxing.

Pierre: If there were opportunity, I will travel to Mount Lushan.

生词 New Words

1.	趟	tàng	m.	used for a round trip, etc.
2.	又	yòu	adv.	again
3.	因为	yīnwèi	conj.	because
4.	所以	suǒyǐ	conj.	so, therefore
5.	地方	dìfang	n.	place
6.	喝	hē	v.	to drink
7.	一边……一边	yìbiān	adv.	indicating two actions taking place at the same time

8. 欣赏	xīnshǎng	v.	to enjoy; to appreciate
9. 休闲	xiūxián	v.	relax
10. 机会	jīhuì	n.	chance; opportunity

Texts 课文 kèwén

美娜：上周末我去了一趟庐山，喝了庐山云雾茶。

荷西：好喝吗？

美娜：太好喝了。我买了两盒，可以给你一盒。

荷西：好啊，谢谢！

美娜：江南，我还想了解更多江西的茶。

江南：江西的茶有很长的历史。江西的很多地方都种茶。

美娜：有哪些茶呢？

江南：有婺源绿茶、修水宁红茶、遂川狗牯脑茶、景德镇浮梁茶等，这些都是很有名的茶。

美娜：江西的茶真多啊。

江南：是啊。江西人喜欢喝茶。以前人们经常一边喝茶一边听戏曲。

美娜：我觉得和好朋友一边喝茶一边聊天儿，非常开心！

English Version

Mena: I went to Mount Lushan last weekend and drank Lushan Yunwu tea.

Jose: Is it good?

Mena: It tastes very good. I've bought two boxes, and I can give you one.

Jose: Thank you very much.

Mena: I would also like to learn more about tea in Jiangxi province.

Jiang Nan: Teas in Jiangxi have a long history. Tea is planted in many places in Jiangxi.

Mena: What kinds of teas?

Jiang Nan: There are Xiushui Ning-Black Tea, Suichuan Gougunao Tea, Jingdezhen Fuliang Tea, etc. These are all famous teas.

Mena: There are so many kinds of teas in Jiangxi!

Jiang Nan: Yeah! Jiangxi people like drinking tea. They used to listening to opera while drinking tea.

Mena: I think it's very happy to chat with good friends while drinking tea!

生词 New Words

1. 太	tài	adv.	too, excessively
2. 一点儿	yìdiǎnr	num.-m.	a few, a little
3. 了解	liǎojiě	v.	to know
4. 更	gèng	adv.	more, even more
5. 长	cháng	adj.	long
6. 种	zhòng	v.	to plant
7. 等	děng	part.	and so on
8. 戏曲	xìqǔ	n.	traditional (Chinese) opera
9. 聊天儿	liáotiānr	v.	to chat
10. 开心	kāixīn	adj.	happy, joyous

Proper Noun 专有名词 Zhuānyǒu míngcí

庐山云雾茶	Lúshān Yúnwùchá	Lushan Yunwu (Cloud and Mist) Tea
婺源绿茶	Wùyuán Lǜchá	Wuyuan Green Tea
修水宁红茶	Xiūshuǐ Nínghóngchá	Xiushui Ning-Black Tea
遂川狗牯脑茶	Suìchuān Gǒugǔ'nǎochá	Suichuan Gougunao Tea
景德镇浮梁茶	Jǐngdézhèn Fúliángchá	Jingdezhen Fuliang Tea

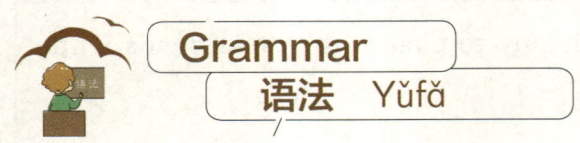

Grammar
语法 Yǔfǎ

1. "又"和"再"　The adverb "又" and "再"

副词"又"和"再"都可以表示动作行为的重复。"又+V"多用于已经发生的情况,"再+V"多用于还没发生的情况。

The adverb "又" and "再" can both indicate the repetition of an action. "又+V" usually indicates the recurrence of an action which has already taken place, while "再+V" usually indicates the recurrence of an action which is yet to take place.

（1）上周末我去了一趟景德镇,昨天又去了一次。

（2）昨天我喝了一杯咖啡,今天又喝了一杯。

（3）庐山云雾茶真好喝,我再喝一杯。

（4）庐山太美了,我想再去一次。

2. 关联词"因为……所以……"　The Pair of Conjunction "因为……所以……"

"因为……所以……"连接一个因果复句。"因为"表示原因,"所以"表示结果。可以成对出现,也可以单独使用。

"因为……所以……" is used to connect two clauses in causative relation. "因为" indicates the cause, while "所以" indicates the effect. They can be used in pair or alone.

（1）因为庐山很漂亮,所以我想去看看。

（2）因为明天我有课,所以不能和你一起去滕王阁。

3. "一边……一边……"　The Structure "一边……一边……"

"一边……一边……"表示两个动作同时进行。可以省略为"边……

边……"。

"一边……一边……" indicates that two actions happen at the same time. Sometimes it can be "边……边……" as well.

（1）我们一边爬山一边聊天儿。

（2）美娜喜欢一边吃南昌炒粉一边喝瓦罐汤。

（3）他边上网边听（music）。

1. 根据课文内容回答下列问题　Answer the questions according to the texts

（1）美娜去过庐山吗？

（2）美娜这次去了庐山的哪些地方？

（3）美娜在庐山喝了什么茶？

（4）江西有哪些茶？

（5）以前江西人喜欢一边喝茶一边干什么？

2. 选词填空　Choose the appropriate words to fill in the blanks

又　　再　　所以　　一边　　了解

（1）我昨天喝了一杯庐山云雾茶，今天还想_____喝一杯。

（2）我早上吃了一碗南昌炒粉，晚上_____吃了一碗。

（3）我喜欢一边喝茶_____看书。

（4）我想_____中国的茶文化。

（5）因为这个周末天气很好，_____我打算去滕王阁玩儿。

3. 组词成句　Make up sentences with the given words

（1）再　景德镇　想　一次　去　我

_____

（2）买　我　茶　了　又　一些

_____

（3）明天　我　一趟　再　超市　去

_____

（4）一边　汉语　我们　历史　了解　一边　学习

_____

4. 交际练习　Communication task

用汉语介绍你喝过的茶。

Please introduce a kind of tea which you have drank before in Chinese.

_____

_____

_____

_____

_____

_____

_____

_____

Cultural Tip
文化贴士　Wénhuà tiēshì

赣茶香天下——江西茶文化

茶是江西人的主要饮品，茶叶生产是江西人的骄傲。"茶圣"陆羽久居江西而著《茶经》。江西产茶历史悠久，远在唐代便吸引了全国茶商。唐代诗人白居易《琵琶行》中"前月浮梁买茶去"描述的正是这一盛况。元明清时期，江西茶不仅被列为贡品，还通过海上丝绸之路出口到欧洲等地。

江西茶以红茶为主，所产红茶根据产地不同而得名，产于修水、武宁等地的，称为"宁红"；产于铅山、上饶等地的，称为"河红"；产于浮梁等地的，称为"祈红"。宁红是中国红茶中的珍品，在海外广受欢迎，英国商人曾赞其"茶盖中华""价甲天下"。此外，江西还有婺源绿茶、庐山云雾茶、遂川狗牯脑茶等绿茶珍品，茶汁芬芳，享誉中外。诗人白居易在品尝了庐山云雾茶后，情不自禁地以诗赞之："匡庐云雾窟，云蒸翠茶复，春来幽香似，岩泉蕊独浓。"

在江西，饮茶不仅是文人雅客的爱好，民间也有着广泛的饮茶习俗。江西人在日常生活中处处离不开茶，家中有喜事时，人们往往在一起饮茶庆祝。茶配以点心，是江西人的传统习惯，故点心又被称为"茶点"。九江茶饼、丰城冻米糖、贵溪灯芯糕、赣南干果等都是极富特色的茶点。时至今日，茶文化成为江西文化的重要组成部分。

Gan Tea Scents the World – Jiangxi Tea Culture

Tea is the main beverage of Jiangxi people, and tea production is the pride of Jiangxi people. Lu Yu, the Saint of Tea, lived in Jiangxi for a long time and wrote the *Tea Classic*. Jiangxi has a long history of tea production, attracting tea merchants from all over the country as far back as the Tang Dynasty. The poet Bai Juyi of the Tang Dynasty, *Pipa Xing*, "the first month to buy tea in Fuliang" describes this flourishing situation. During the Yuan, Ming and Qing dynasties, Jiangxi tea was not only paid as tribute, but also exported to Europe through the Maritime Silk Road.

Jiangxi tea is mainly black tea, the black tea produced according to the origin of different names, produced in Xiushui, Wuning and other places, known as "Ning Hong"; produced in Lingshan, Shangrao and other places, known as "He red"; produced in Fuliang and other places, known as "Qi Hong". Ning Hong is a rare Chinese black tea, popular overseas, British merchants have praised its "tea cover China", "price A world". In addition, Jiangxi has Wuyuan green tea, Lushan Yunwu tea, Suichuan Gougunao tea and other green tea treasures, tea juice fragrant, well-known in China and abroad. The poet Bai Juyi in a taste of Mount Lushan cloud tea, can not help but praise the poem: "There are a lot of clouds and Mist in Mount Lushan, and the mist makes the tea leaves extra green. In the spring Mount Lushan's tea fragrance overflowing, the mountain spring water are as if nectar as sweet."

In Jiangxi, drinking tea is not only the hobby of the literati and elegant guests, folk also have a wide range of tea drinking customs. Jiangxi people can not live without tea everywhere in their daily lives, when there are happy events at home, people often celebrate together with tea. Tea with snacks is a traditional custom of Jiangxi people, so the snacks are also known as "tea points". Jiujiang tea cakes, Fengcheng frozen rice candy, Guixi lamp core cake, Gannan dried fruit, etc. are all very special tea points. To this day, tea culture has become an important part of Jiangxi culture.

第六课　江西的戏曲越听越好听
LESSON 6　The more I listen to Jiangxi opera, the better it sounds

- 知识目标：掌握"A跟B一样""虽然……但是……""越A越B"的用法
- 能力目标：能够用汉语对比不同事物、表达对某事物的看法
- 文化目标：了解江西的戏曲文化

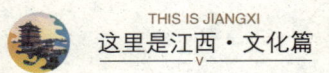

第六课　江西的戏曲越听越好听

Key Sentences
重点句　Zhòngdiǎn jù

1. 跟京剧一样吗？　　　　　Gēn Jīngjù yíyàng ma?
2. 我越听越喜欢。　　　　　Wǒ yuè tīng yuè xǐhuan.
3. 虽然很难，但是我　　　　Suīrán hěn nán, dànshì wǒ
   也要坚持学。　　　　　　yě yào jiānchí xué.

Warm-up
热身　Rèshēn

说一说你知道的中国戏曲。

Talk about the Chinese opera you know.

Jīngjù
京剧

Kūnqǔ
昆曲

Huángméixì
黄梅戏

Gànjù
赣剧

第六课　江西的戏曲越听越好听
LESSON 6 The more I listen to Jiangxi opera, the better it sounds

Cǎicháxì
采茶戏

Yìyángqiāng
弋阳腔

Texts
课文　kèwén

Jiāng Nán: Nǐ xǐhuan tīng yīnyuè ma?
江　南：你 喜欢 听 音乐 吗？

Měinà: Dāngrán xǐhuan.
美娜：当然 喜欢。

Jiāng Nán: Nǐ zhīdào Jiāngxī de xìqǔ ma?
江　南：你 知道 江西 的 戏曲 吗？

Měinà: Bù zhīdào, gēn Jīngjù yíyàng ma?
美娜：不 知道，跟 京剧 一样 吗？

Jiāng Nán: Bù yíyàng. Jiāngxī de xìqǔ yǒu hěn duō zhǒnglèi, bǐrú Gànjù,
江　南：不 一样。江西 的 戏曲 有 很 多 种类，比如 赣剧、

　　　　　Cǎicháxì, Yìyángqiāng děng.
　　　　　采茶戏、弋阳腔 等。

Měinà: Nǐ xǐhuan tīng nǎ yì zhǒng?
美娜：你 喜欢 听 哪 一 种？

Jiāng Nán: Wǒ chángcháng tīng Cǎicháxì, hěn yǒu yìsi.
江　南：我 常常 听 采茶戏，很 有 意思。

Měinà: Wǒ yídìng yào tīngting.
美娜：我 一定 要 听听。

Jiāng Nán: Zhè ge zhōumò yǒu Cǎicháxì de biǎoyǎn, wǒmen yìqǐ qù
江　南：这 个 周末 有 采茶戏 的 表演，我们 一起 去

　　　　　tīngting ba.
　　　　　听听 吧。

Měinà: Tài hǎo le!
美娜：太 好 了！

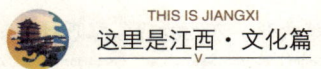
这里是江西·文化篇

English Version

Jiang Nan: Do you like to listen to music?

Mena: Of course.

Jiang Nan: Do you know about operas in Jiangxi?

Mena: I do not know. Are they the same as Beijing Opera?

Jiang Nan: No, they are different. There are many types of operas in Jiangxi, such as Gan Opera, Tea-picking Opera, Yiyang Opera, etc.

Mena: Which type do you prefer?

Jiang Nan: I often listen to Tea-picking Opera, it is very interesting.

Mena: I will definitely listen to it.

Jiang Nan: There is a Tea-picking Opera show this weekend, let's go to see together.

Mena: That's nice!

生词 New Words

1. 知道	zhīdào	v.	to know
2. 跟	gēn	prep.	with
3. 一样	yíyàng	adj.	same, as…as…
4. 种类	zhǒnglèi	n.	kind, variety
5. 比如	bǐrú	v.	for example
6. 人们	rénmen	n.	people
7. 采	cǎi	v.	to pick

第六课　江西的戏曲越听越好听
LESSON 6 The more I listen to Jiangxi opera, the better it sounds

| 8. 表演 | biǎoyǎn | n. | performance, show |
| 9. 当然 | dāngrán | adv. | of course, certainly |

Texts
课文　kèwén

荷西：你的衣服真漂亮！这是什么衣服？
（Nǐ de yīfu zhēn piàoliang! Zhè shì shénme yīfu?）

美娜：谢谢！这是采茶戏的衣服。我昨天和江南一起去听了采茶戏。
（Xièxie! Zhè shì Cǎicháxì de yīfu. Wǒ zuótiān hé JiāngNán yì qǐ qùtīng le Cǎicháxì.）

荷西：好听吗？
（Hǎotīng ma?）

美娜：好听。虽然我还听不懂，但是越听越好听，我越听越喜欢。你听一下。
（Hǎotīng. Suīrán wǒ hái tīng bu dǒng, dànshì yuè tīng yuè hǎotīng, wǒ yuè tīng yuè xǐhuan. Nǐ tīng yí xià.）

荷西：很特别，跟我们国家的音乐一样好听。
（Hěn tèbié, gēn wǒmen guójiā de yīnyuè yíyàng hǎotīng.）

美娜：我最近在跟老师学采茶戏。
（Wǒ zuìjìn zài gēn lǎoshī xué Cǎicháxì.）

荷西：难吗？
（Nán ma?）

	Měinà:	Yǒudiǎnr nán. Suīrán hěn nán, dànshì wǒ yě yào jiānchí xué.
	美娜：	有点儿难。虽然很难，但是我也要坚持学。

Wǒ juéde yuè xué yuè yǒu yìsi.
我觉得越学越有意思。

Héxī: Jiāyóu!
荷西：加油！

English Version

Jose: Your dress is so beautiful! What kind of dress is this?

Mena: This is the dress for the Tea-picking opera. I went to see the Tea-picking Opera show with Jiang Nan yesterday.

Jose: Is it good?

Mena: I can't understand it completely, but the more I listen to it, the more I like it. Listen.

Jose: Very special, as good as our country's music.

Mena: I'm learning Tea-picking Opera with my teacher recently.

Jose: Is it difficult?

Mena: A little difficult. Although it's hard, I'll keep learning. The more I learn, I feel it more interesting.

Jose: Work harder!

生词　New Words

1. 衣服	yīfu	n.	clothes
2. 虽然	suīrán	conj.	although, though
3. 懂	dǒng	v.	to understand, to know
4. 越	yuè	adv.	more, to a greater degree

第六课　江西的戏曲越听越好听
LESSON 6　The more I listen to Jiangxi opera, the better it sounds

5. 特别	tèbié	adj.&adv.	❶special; ❷very
6. 国家	guójiā	n.	country, nation
7. 最近	zuìjìn	n.	lately, recently
8. 坚持	jiānchí	v.	to persist in, to insist on
9. 加油	jiāyóu	v.	to cheer

Proper Noun
专有名词　Zhuānyǒu míngcí

赣剧	Gànjù	Gan Opera
采茶戏	Cǎicháxì	Tea-picking Opera
弋阳腔	Yìyángqiāng	Yiyang Opera; Yiyang Tune
京剧	Jīngjù	Beijing Opera

Grammar
语法　Yǔfǎ

1. "A 跟 B 一样"　Comparative Sentence "A 跟 B 一样"

"A 跟 B 一样"表示 A、B 两者相比较，结果相同。后面加上形容词可以表示具体比较的方面。否定形式是在"一样"前加"不"。

"A 跟 B 一样" indicates A and B are the same after comparison. An adjective can be added after "一样" to indicate the specific aspects of the comparison. In the negative form, "不" is added before "一样".

（1）这杯茶跟那杯茶一样。

（2）庐山跟婺源一样漂亮。

（3）你们国家的音乐跟我们的不一样。

2. "越 A 越 B" The Structure "越 A 越 B"

"越 A 越 B"表示 B 随着 A 的变化而变化。A 和 B 的主语可以相同，也可以不同。

"越 A 越 B"（the more A, the more B）means B changes with A. A and B can have the same or different subjects.

（1）你的汉语越说越好。

（2）江西菜越吃越好吃。

（3）你越介绍庐山云雾茶，我越想喝。

3. 虽然……但是…… The Pair of Conjunctions "虽然……但是……"

"虽然……但是……"连接两个分句，表示一种转折关系。

"虽然……但是……" is used to connect two clauses, indicating an adversative relation.

（1）汉语虽然很难，但是很有意思。

（2）虽然江西菜很辣，但是我觉得很好吃。

（3）虽然庐山离南昌有点儿远，但是我还是想去那儿玩。

Exercise
练习 Liànxí

1. 根据课文内容回答下列问题 Answer the questions according to the texts

第六课　江西的戏曲越听越好听

LESSON 6　The more I listen to Jiangxi opera, the better it sounds

（1）江西的戏曲跟京剧一样吗？

（2）江西的戏曲有哪些种类？

（3）以前采茶戏是什么时候唱的？

（4）这个周末江南和美娜要去看什么表演？

（5）荷西觉得采茶戏怎么样？

2. 用本课新学的语言点完成句子　Complete the sentences using the newly learned language points

（1）这家商店跟那家商店_____。

（2）赣剧跟采茶戏_____。

（3）江西菜越吃_____。

（4）这本书我越看_____。

（5）虽然庐山有点儿远，_____。

（6）_____，但是我喜欢吃。

3. 组词成句　Make up sentences with the given words

（1）风景　　不一样　　庐山的　　跟　　三清山的

_____

（2）好喝　　越　　庐山云雾茶　　喝　　越

_____

（3）辣　　但是　　很　　江西菜　　虽然　　好吃

_____

4. 交际练习　Communication task

用汉语介绍一种你们国家的戏剧。

Please introduce one opera in your country in Chinese.

Cultural Tip
文化贴士　Wénhuà tiēshì

戏韵传情——江西戏曲

钟灵毓秀的江西，灿烂的戏曲文化曾星光熠熠、惊艳一时。江西的地方戏曲经过数百年的兴替，形成了以赣剧、采茶戏为代表的十余种地方戏种，留下了众多的戏剧历史遗存和人文景观。

赣剧是江西的主要剧种，流行于江西东北一带，前身是饶河班和信河班。赣剧的声腔前期以弋阳腔[①]为主，后期吸纳了昆腔、乱弹腔等，成为具有地方特色的多声腔的剧种。赣剧表演内容多为百姓所喜闻乐见的神话故事和历史传说，如《岳飞传》《西游记》《水浒传》《三国传》等，唱词浅显易懂，在民间广为传唱。弋阳腔是南戏流传到江西弋阳县后形成的，因其高亢激越，又名高腔。弋阳腔在江西产生后，流传到各地，又演变为

---

① 根据《中国戏曲音乐集成·江西卷》，"弋阳腔"这一概念既可指声腔，也可指演唱这种腔调的地方戏。

具有各地特色的新腔，如青阳腔、广腔、京腔等，这些统称为弋阳腔系统，成为中国戏曲四大声腔之一。

采茶戏是江西最有特色的剧种之一，它的发展与江西茶文化密不可分。自唐代以来，江西即是我国主要的产茶区之一，茶叶产地遍及全省，茶区普遍流行采茶歌。采茶戏由采茶歌发展而来，融民间口头文学、民间歌舞、灯彩于一体，具有浓郁的生活气息。

An Opera with Strong Sense of Life—Jiangxi opera

The splendid opera culture of Jiangxi, with its rich and beautiful spirit, was once astonishing. Over the centuries, Jiangxi's local opera has evolved into more than ten types of local opera, represented by Gan Opera and Tea-picking Opera, leaving behind numerous historical and cultural legacies of theatre.

Gan opera is a major drama genre in Jiangxi, popular in the northeast of the country, formerly known as Raohe Ban and Xinhe Ban. The vocal cadences of Ganju were predominantly Yiyang cadences. It is mainly composed of the Kun cadence and the jumbled bomb cadence, and has become a multi-voiced genre with local characteristics. The content of Gan opera is mostly mythological stories and historical legends that are popular among the people, such as "The Legend of Yue Fei", "Journey to the West", "The Legend of Water Margin" and "The Legend of the Three Kingdoms", etc. The lyrics are easy to understand and are widely sung among the people. The Yiyang cadence was formed after the southern opera was spread to Yiyang County, Jiangxi, and is also known as the high cadence because of its high and aggressive tone. After it arose in Jiangxi, the Yiyang cadence spread to different parts of the country and evolved into new cadences with local characteristics, such as the Qingyang cadence, the Guang cadence and the Jing cadence, which are collectively known as the Yiyang cadence system and have become one of the four major vocal cadences of Chinese opera.

Tea-picking opera is one of the most distinctive types of opera in Jiangxi, and its development is inseparable from Jiangxi's tea culture. Since the Tang Dynasty, Jiangxi is one of the main tea-producing areas in China, tea production areas throughout the province, tea picking songs are popular in tea areas. Tea picking opera from the development of tea songs, folk oral literature, folk songs and dances, lanterns in one, with a strong sense of life.

第七课　我把八大山人纪念馆逛完了

LESSON 7　I finished visiting the Badashanren Memorial Hall

- 知识目标：掌握"把"字句和"先……，再/又……，然后……"的基本用法
- 能力目标：能够自主参观中国的景点
- 文化目标：了解八大山人生平及作品

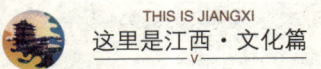

第七课　我把八大山人纪念馆逛完了

Key Sentences
重点句　Zhòngdiǎn jù

1. 请把你的护照给我看看。　　Qǐng bǎ nǐ de hùzhào gěi wǒ kànkan.
2. 我们先逛了一楼，　　　　　Wǒmen xiān guàng le yī lóu,
   又逛了二楼。　　　　　　　yòu guàng le èr lóu.
3. 要先看你的护照，　　　　　Yào xiān kàn nǐ de hùzhào,
   然后才能进去。　　　　　　ránhòu cái néng jìnqu.

Warm-up
热身　Rèshēn

说一说，这些画里都有什么？

Talk about what are they in the pictures below.

niǎo
鸟

māo
猫

yú
鱼

lù
鹿

hé huā
荷花

yīng
鹰

Texts
课文　kèwén

Lǐ Yáng: Nǐ kàn, zhè jiù shì Bādàshānrén Jìniànguǎn.
李阳：你看，这就是八大山人纪念馆。

Pí'āi'ěr: Zhèr yǒu shuǐ, yǒu shù, zhēn piàoliang!
皮埃尔：这儿有水、有树，真漂亮！

Gōngzuòrényuán: Qǐng bǎ nǐ de hùzhào gěi wǒ kànkan.
工作人员：请把你的护照给我看看。

皮埃尔：好的。哎，我的护照呢？

李阳：你把它放在哪儿了？

皮埃尔：我记得我把它放在书包里了，但是没有找到。

李阳：别着急，再找一找。有没有在你的口袋里？

皮埃尔：真的在这儿！我什么时候把护照放在口袋里了？给您！

工作人员：可以进去了。食物不可以带进去，请把食物放在那边的柜子里。

李阳：知道了，谢谢！

English Version

Li Yang: Look, this is the Badashanren Memorial Hall.

Pierre: There's water and trees here. How beautiful it is!

Staff: Please show me your passport.

Pierre: Okay. Opps! Where's my passport?

Li Yang: Where did you put it?

Pierre: I remember I put it in my schoolbag, but it isn't there.

第七课　我把八大山人纪念馆逛完了
LESSON 7　I finished visiting the Badashanren Memorial Hall

Li Yang: Don't worry, look for it again. Is it in your pocket?

Pierre: Here it is! When did I put my passport in my pocket? Here you are!

Staff: You can go inside now. No food allowed. Please put them in the cupboard over there.

生词　*New Words*

1.	水	shuǐ	n.	water
2.	树	shù	n.	tree
3.	把	bǎ	prep.	（used in the "把" sentence）denoting the disposal of something
4.	记得	jìde	v.	to remember
5.	别	bié	adv.	don't
6.	着急	zháojí	adj.	worry, anxious
7.	口袋	kǒudài	n.	pocket
8.	里	lǐ	n.	inside
9.	放	fàng	v.	to put
10.	柜子	guìzi	n.	cupboard, cabinet

Texts
课文 kèwén

荷西：皮埃尔，你们今天玩得怎么样？

皮埃尔：我们把八大山人纪念馆逛完了，那儿又大又漂亮，两层楼都是画儿。

荷西：那么多画儿你们都看完了吗？

皮埃尔：对啊，我们先逛了一楼，又逛了二楼，才把那些画儿看完。我发现，八大山人的画儿特别有意思！

荷西：八大山人是谁？是八个画家吗？

皮埃尔：不是，八大山人其实是一个人。他是中国古代很有名的画家。他的画儿跟别人的画儿不一样，很有自己的特色。

荷西：是吗？有什么特色？

皮埃尔：他画的鸟、鱼等都闭着眼睛或者眼睛看天，他画的花草和石头看起来又孤独又骄傲。

荷西：真有意思，我也想去看看他的画儿。

第七课　我把八大山人纪念馆逛完了

LESSON 7 I finished visiting the Badashanren Memorial Hall

Pí'āi'ěr: Nà nǐ bié wàng le bǎ hùzhào dài shàng, yào xiān kàn nǐ de hùzhào, ránhòu cái néng jìnqu.

皮埃尔：那你别忘了把护照带上，要先看你的护照，然后才能进去。

English Version

Jose: Pierre, how is your visiting today?

Pierre: I finished visiting the Badashanren Memorial Hall. It was big and beautiful, with two floors of paintings.

Jose: Have you seen all those paintings?

Pierre: Yes, we went to the first floor first, then the second floor. I found the Badashanren's paintings are very interesting!

Jose: Who are the Badashanren? Are they eight painters?

Pierre: No, Badashanren is actually one person. He is a famous painter in ancient China. His paintings are different from others' and have his own characteristics.

Jose: Really? What are the features?

Pierre: The birds, fish,etc, in his paintings either close their eyes or look up at the sky. The flowers and stones in his paintings seem to be lonely and proud.

Jose: That's interesting. I'd like to see his paintings, too.

Pierre: Then don't forget to take your passport with you. Need to check your passport first, and then let you in.

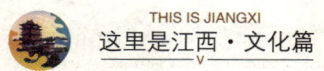

生词 New Words

1. 逛	guàng	v.	to stroll, to wander
2. 完	wán	v.	to finish
3. 古代	gǔdài	n.	ancient times
4. 画家	huàjiā	n.	painter
5. 鸟	niǎo	n.	bird
6. 闭	bì	v.	to close, to shut
7. 眼睛	yǎnjing	n.	eye
8. 草	cǎo	n.	grass
9. 石头	shítou	n.	stone
10. 孤独	gūdú	adj.	lonely
11. 骄傲	jiāoào	adj.	pride, proud

Proper Noun
专有名词 Zhuānyǒu míngcí

八大山人	Bādàshānrén	a famous painter in Ming Dynasty

Grammar
语法 Yǔfǎ

1. "把"字句 The "把" sentence

"把"字句是汉语中一种特殊句式,它常常用来表示通过某种动作对某些已知的人或者事物进行相应的处置，或使其位置发生变化等。

The "把" sentence is a special sentence pattern in Chinese, which is frequently used in Chinese to indicate the corresponding disposal of some known people or things or the position change of them through certain actions, and so on.

Subject	Predicate			
	把	O	V	other elements
他	把	这件事	忘	了
我	把	饭	吃	完了
妈妈	把	碗	洗	干净了
皮埃尔	把	护照	放	在书包里了

"把"字句的否定句应把否定副词放在"把"字的前面。

The negative pattern of the "把" sentence should put the negative adverb in front of the word "把".

（1）你别把这件事忘了。

（2）我不想把手机给你。

（3）皮埃尔没把护照放在书包里。

2. 先……，再/又……，然后…… The usage of "先……，再/又……，然后……"

汉语中，用"先……，再/又……，然后……"来表示动作发生的先后顺序。其中"再"表示动作还没有发生，而"又"表示动作已经发生了。

In Chinese, "先……，再/又……，然后……" indicates the order in which a series of actions take place. In that structure, "再" indicates the action has not taken place, and "又" indicates the action has already taken place.

（1）我们先逛一楼，再逛二楼。

（2）要先看你的护照，然后才能进去。

（3）我先到了南昌，又去了庐山，然后去了婺源。

1. 根据课文内容回答下列问题　Answer the following questions according to the texts

（1）李阳和皮埃尔去哪儿了？

（2）皮埃尔觉得那个地方怎么样？

（3）皮埃尔把护照放在哪儿了？

（4）八大山人是谁？

（5）八大山人的画儿有什么特色？

2. 替换练习　Substitution drills

（1）我把<u>护照</u>　<u>放在口袋里</u>了。

　　　书包　　放在教室里

　　　饺子　　吃完

　　　护照　　给老师

（2）<u>我们先逛了一楼，然后逛了二楼</u>。

　　　我　　吃饭　　喝汤

　　　同学们　　学生词　　学课文

　　　皮埃尔　　去婺源　　去樟树

（3）别忘了<u>把护照带上</u>。

　　　打电话给我

　　　买火车票

晚上一起看电影（film）

3. 组词成句　Make up sentences with the given words

（1）忘了　吃　别　晚饭

_____

（2）把　了　你　放　护照　在哪儿

_____

（3）给　她　了　作业　老师　把

_____

（4）喝　瓦罐汤　把　美娜　了　完

_____

4. 交际练习　Communication task

上网查一查八大山人的介绍和他的绘画作品，说一说你的认识。

Look up the introduction of Badashanren and his paintings on the Internet, and tell each other what you know.

_____

_____

_____

_____

_____

隐逸画宗——八大山人

八大山人是清代著名书画家朱耷（1626—1705）的别号之一。朱耷，江西南昌人，明朝皇室后裔，明末清初的著名书画家。朱耷从小就受到艺术陶冶，八岁能作诗，十一岁能作画。为了躲避清初的政治纷争，八大山人出家为僧，后在青云谱道观隐居。

八大山人在绘画、书法、诗跋、篆刻等方面有着很高的造诣，尤其以绘画上的成就最高。八大山人以大写意花鸟画著称，其风格承袭了明代画家董其昌、徐渭等人的传统，将其发展为阔笔大写意的画法：画鸟兽虫鱼，大都形象怪诞，将鸟、鱼等画成"白眼向天"的姿态；画花卉，多写芭蕉、枯荷、古松；画山水，大都是荒岭怪石，表现了"残山剩水，地寒天荒"的境界。这些画作中表现出八大山人孤傲不群、愤世嫉俗的个性。

八大山人在继承前人传统的基础上，发展出独树一帜、简约沉郁的画风。清代中期的"扬州八怪"、晚期的"海派"以及近代的齐白石、张大千、李苦禅等巨匠均受其影响，对他极为推崇。郑板桥在其画上题"八大名满天下"，吴昌硕曾赞其"高古超逸，无溢笔无赘笔"。

Bada Shanren, the Patriarch of Hermitage Painting

Bada Shanren (1626–1705) is one of the aliases of Zhu Da, a famous calligrapher and painter of the Qing Dynasty. Zhu Da, born in Nanchang, Jiangxi Province, was a descendant of the Ming Dynasty royal family and a famous calligrapher and painter in the late Ming and early Qing dynasties. Zhu Da was trained in art since childhood, and could compose poems at the age of eight and paint at the age of eleven. In order to escape the political strife of the early Qing Dynasty, Bada Shanren became a monk and later lived in seclusion at the Qingyunpu Taoist temple.

Bada Shanren had high attainments in painting, calligraphy, poetry and seal carving, especially in painting. His style inherited the tradition of Ming Dynasty painters such as Dong Qichang and Xu Wei, and developed it into a broad brush painting method: painting birds, animals, insects and fish, most of them are grotesque, and the birds and fish are painted in the posture of "white eyes to the sky"; painting flowers, most of them are bananas, withered lotus, and ancient pines; painting landscapes, most of them are wild mountains and strange rocks. The paintings of flowers are mostly about bananas, withered lotus and ancient pines, while the landscapes are mostly about strange rocks and mountains. These paintings show Bada Shanren's solitary and cynical personality.

Based on the tradition of his predecessors, Bada Shanren developed a unique, simple and somber style of painting. The "Eight Monsters of Yangzhou" in the mid-Qing Dynasty, the "Sea School" in the late Qing Dynasty, and the giants Qi Baishi, Zhang Daqian and Li Kuchan in modern times were all influenced by him and held him in high esteem. Zheng Banqiao inscribed on his paintings "Bada with Great Fame", and Wu Changshuo praised him for his "high ancient and superb, without overflowing or superfluous strokes."

第八课　白鹿洞书院有一千年左右的历史

LESSON 8 Bailudong Academy has a history of about one thousand years

- 知识目标：掌握用"左右"表达概数的用法、疑问代词的活用
- 能力目标：能够用汉语简单地描述一个地方、表达兴趣
- 文化目标：了解白鹿洞书院和书院文化

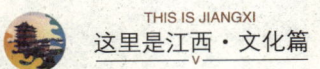

第八课　白鹿洞书院有一千年左右的历史

Key Sentences
重点句　Zhòngdiǎn jù

1. 我对中国的书院文化很感兴趣。　Wǒ duì Zhōngguó de shūyuàn wénhuà hěn gǎn xìngqù.
2. 白鹿洞书院有一千年左右的历史。　Báilùdòng shūyuàn yǒu yìqiān nián zuǒyòu de lìshǐ.
3. 我哪天都可以。　Wǒ nǎ tiān dōu kěyǐ.

Warm-up
热身　Rèshēn

你了解中国古代的书院吗？

Do you know the ancient academy in China?

Sōngyáng shūyuàn
嵩阳　书院

Yuèlù shūyuàn
岳麓　书院

第八课　白鹿洞书院有一千年左右的历史
LESSON 8 Bailudong Academy has a history of about one thousand years

Yīngtiānfǔ shūyuàn
应天府　书院

Báilùdòng shūyuàn
白鹿洞　书院

Éhú shūyuàn
鹅湖　书院

Xiàngshān shūyuàn
象山　书院

Texts
课文　kèwén

A

荷西：Wǒ tīngshuō Zhōngguó yǒu wǔqiān duō nián de lìshǐ, shì zhēnde ma?
我 听说 中国 有 五千 多 年 的 历史，是 真的 吗？

李阳：Duì, Zhōngguó de lìshǐ hěn yōujiǔ.
对，中国 的 历史 很 悠久。

荷西：Wǒ duì Zhōngguó de shūyuàn wénhuà hěn gǎn xìngqù.
我 对 中国 的 书院 文化 很 感 兴趣。

李阳：Zhōngguó yǒu sì gè hěn yǒumíng de shūyuàn, qízhōng yí gè zài Jiāngxī, nǐ zhīdào shì nǎge ma?
中国 有 四 个 很 有名 的 书院，其中 一 个 在 江西，你 知道 是 哪个 吗？

荷西：Shì Báilùdòng shūyuàn.
是 白鹿洞 书院。

李阳：Duì, érqiě Báilùdòng shūyuàn shì Zhōngguó zuì yǒumíng de
对，而且 白鹿洞 书院 是 中国 最 有名 的

                shūyuàn. Tā zài Jiāngxī Shěng Jiǔjiāng Shì, Lúshān jiǎo xià.
                书院。它 在 江西 省 九江 市，庐山 脚 下。

Héxī：Tā yǒu duōshao nián de   lìshǐ?
荷西：它 有 多少 年 的 历史？

Lǐ Yáng：Tā yǒu yìqiān nián zuǒyòu de lìshǐ.
李 阳：它 有 一千 年 左右 的 历史。

Héxī：Wā！Nǐ shénme shíhou yǒu shíjiān？ Péi wǒ qù kànkan ba.
荷西：哇！你 什么 时候 有 时间？陪 我 去 看看 吧。

Lǐ Yáng：Hǎo a！Xià zhōu fàngjià, wǒ nǎ tiān dōu kěyǐ.
李 阳：好 啊！下 周 放假，我 哪 天 都 可以。

English Version

Jose: I heard that China has a history of more than 5,000 years, is it true?

Li Yang: Yes, China has a long history.

Jose: I am very interested in Chinese academy culture.

Li Yang: There are four famous academies in China, one of them is in Jiangxi Province. Do you know which one it is?

Jose: It is Bailudong Academy.

Li Yang: Yes, Bailudong Academy is the most famous academy in China. It is located in Jiujiang City, Jiangxi Province, at the foot of Wulao Peak.

Jose: How long is the history of it?

Li Yang: It has a history of about one thousand years.

Jose: Wow! When do you have time? Will you come with me to see it?

Li Yang: Okay! Next week is a holiday. Either day of the next week is fine for me.

第八课 白鹿洞书院有一千年左右的历史
LESSON 8 Bailudong Academy has a history of about one thousand years

生词 New Words

1. 左右	zuǒyòu	n.	(used after a numeral) about; around
2. 对	duì	prep.&adj.	❶(used before a noun or pronoun) to, for; ❷ right
3. 文化	wénhuà	n.	culture
4. 感兴趣	gǎn xìngqù		to be interested in
5. 其中	qízhōng	n.	among
6. 省	shěng	n.	province
7. 市	shì	n.	city
8. 脚	jiǎo	n.	foot
9. 陪	péi	v.	to accompany

Texts
课文 kèwén

Lǐ Yáng: Zǒu, wǒmen jìnqu ba.
李阳：走，我们进去吧。

HéXī: Shūyuàn li zhēn ānjìng.
荷西：书院里真安静。

Li Yang: Shì a, shūyuàn li nǎr dōu hěn ānjìng.
李阳：是啊，书院里哪儿都很安静。

HéXī: Zhèli búdàn ānjìng, érqiě huánjìng yě hěn hǎo, yǒu huā, yǒu
荷西：这里不但安静，而且环境也很好，有花、有

Lǐ Yáng: ... cǎo, kōngqì yě hěn xīnxiān.
草，空气也很新鲜。

Lǐ Yáng: Báilùdòng shūyuàn zhème yǒumíng, hé yí gè rén yǒuguān.
李阳：白鹿洞书院这么有名，和一个人有关。

HéXī: Shì shéi a?
荷西：是谁啊？

Lǐ Yáng: Tā jiào Zhū Xī, shì NánSòng de dà xuézhě, céngjīng zài zhèli jiǎng kè.
李阳：他叫朱熹，是南宋的大学者，曾经在这里讲课。

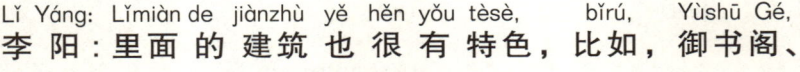

HéXī: Wǒ yòu zhīdào le yí gè lìshǐ rénwù.
荷西：我又知道了一个历史人物。

Lǐ Yáng: Lǐmiàn de jiànzhù yě hěn yǒu tèsè, bǐrú, Yùshū Gé, Mínglún Táng, Sīxián Tái, Zhūzǐ Cí děng.
李阳：里面的建筑也很有特色，比如，御书阁、明伦堂、思贤台、朱子祠等。

HéXī: Yìbiān cānguān shūyuàn yìbiān liǎojiě lìshǐ, zhēn shì tài hǎo le! Wǒ yào bǎ tāmen dōu guàng wán.
荷西：一边参观书院一边了解历史，真是太好了！我要把它们都逛完。

Lǐ Yáng: Guàng wán yào yì tiān zuǒyòu.
李阳：逛完要一天左右。

HéXī: Nà wǒmen kuài guàng ba.
荷西：那我们快逛吧。

English Version

Li Yang: Come on, let's go inside.

Jose: It's so quiet in this academy.

Li Yang: Yes, everywhere here is very quiet.

Jose: Here is not only quiet, but also has an good environment.

第八课　白鹿洞书院有一千年左右的历史
LESSON 8 Bailudong Academy has a history of about one thousand years

There are flowers, grass and fresh air.

Li Yang: It is because a man that Bailudong academy become famous.

Jose: Who is that?

Li Yang: His name is Zhu Xi. He is a great scholar of the Southern Song Dynasty and once gave lectures here.

Jose: I see. I have learned one more historical figure.

Li Yang: The buildings inside are also very distinctive, such as Yushu Pavilion, Minglun Hall, Sixian Pavilion, Zhizi Memorial temple and so on.

Jose: It was great to learn about the history while visiting the academy! I'm going to look around the whole academy.

Li Yang: It takes about one day to finish the sightseeing.

Jose: Let's get start now.

生词　*New Words*

1. 安静	ānjìng	adj.	quiet
2. 环境	huánjìng	n.	environment
3. 空气	kōngqì	n.	air; atmosphere
4. 新鲜	xīnxiān	adj.	fresh
5. 有关	yǒuguān	v.	to be relevant, about
6. 学者	xuézhě	n.	scholar
7. 曾经	céngjīng	adv.	ever; once
8. 讲课	jiǎng kè	v.	to give a lecture

9. 人物	rénwù	n.	person of distinction; character in works of literature and art
10. 建筑	jiànzhù	n.	architecture
11. 快	kuài	adj.	quickly

Proper Noun
专有名词 Zhuānyǒu míngcí

朱熹	Zhū Xī	a philosopher in the Southern Song Dynasty
南宋	Nán Sòng	the Southern Song Dynasty（1127–1279）
御书阁	Yùshū Gé	Yushu Pavilion
明伦堂	Mínglún Táng	Minglun Hall
思贤台	Sīxián Tái	Sixian Terrace
朱子祠	Zhūzǐ Cí	Zhuzi Memorial Temple

Grammar
语法 Yǔfǎ

1. 概数的表达：左右   Expression of Approximate Number：左右

"左右"用在数量词语后表示概数，指比这一数量稍多或稍少。

"左右" indicates an approximate number after a numeral, means "a little more than or less than the mentioned amount."

（1）一碗南昌炒粉八块钱左右。

（2）我们在秋水广场玩了一个小时左右。

（3）我们走了 10 分钟左右。

2. 疑问代词的活用　Flexible Use of Interrogative Pronouns

"谁""什么""怎么""哪儿"等疑问代词可代替某个范围内的每一个对象，用来表示它们都有相同的情况。

Interrogative pronouns such as "谁", "什么", "怎么" and "哪儿" can be used to refer every member within a certain range, indicating all of them are the same in a certain way.

（1）什么江西菜我都想尝尝。

（2）江西哪儿我都想去。

（3）你想怎么去婺源都可以。

3. 表达兴趣　To Express an Interest

汉语中，通常用"对……感兴趣"和"对……有兴趣"表达兴趣。否定式是"对……不感兴趣"和"对……没（有）兴趣"。

In Chinese, "对……感兴趣" or "对……有兴趣" are usually used to express interest. The negative form is "对……不感兴趣" or "对……没（有）兴趣."

（1）我对中国文化感兴趣。

（2）我对江西的历史很感兴趣。

（3）以前我对戏曲不感兴趣，现在非常感兴趣。

Exercise 练习 Liànxí

1. 根据课文内容回答下列问题　Answer the questions according to the texts

（1）中国最有名的书院是哪个书院？

（2）它有多少年的历史？

（3）南宋的哪位大学者曾经在这里讲课？

（4）白鹿洞书院里面有什么建筑？

2. 根据提示完成句子或对话　Complete the sentences using the expressions provided

（1）我们在庐山_____。（左右）

（2）中国_____都_____。（哪儿）

（3）景德镇的瓷器_____都_____。（谁）

（4）我_____。（对……感兴趣）

3. 组词成句　Make up sentences with the given words

（1）我　了　左右　逛　小时　两个

_____

（2）我　可以　去　白鹿洞书院　都　哪天

_____

（3）茶文化　对　我　感兴趣　中国的

_____

4. 交际练习　Communication task

用汉语介绍一个你去过的景点。

Please introduce a famous scenic spot in China where you ever been in Chinese.

_____

_____

_____

_____

_____

_____

_____

_____

_____

_____

Cultural Tip
文化贴士　Wénhuà tiēshì

林泉学府——白鹿洞书院

书院是中国古代教育机构。江西古代书院文化发达，不仅是中国古代书院文化的发祥地，而且数量之多居全国各省之首。根据学者统计，江西历代共有书院 990 所，约占全国的七分之一[①]。江西书院的学规之完备、办学质量之高，为时人交口称赞。白鹿洞书院成为全国四大书院之首，其他如鹅湖书院、白鹭洲书院、象山书院等在全国亦享有盛名。

白鹿洞书院创建于晚唐，重建于南宋，沿袭到明清，已有 1000 多年历史，有"天下书院之首""海内书院第一"的美誉。著名儒家学者朱熹、陆九渊、王阳明等都曾在此讲学。

白鹿洞书院之所以成为天下书院之首，与朱熹是分不开的。朱熹为重建白鹿洞书院投入了大量精力，不仅亲自讲学，还制定了《白鹿洞书院揭示》，明确了教育的目的，提出了修身、处事、接物的基本要求。

《白鹿洞书院揭示》成为各地书院共同遵循的学规，明清时期又传到朝鲜、日本等地。朝鲜深受中国书院的影响，在白鹿洞书院的影响下，建立了白云洞书院。《白鹿洞书院学规》至今仍悬挂在韩国绍修书院、陶山书院的讲堂之上。在部分日本与韩国的乡校，现在仍有集体吟诵《白鹿洞书院揭示》的活动。

---

① 袁行霈，陈进玉主编．《中国地域文化通览：江西卷》[M]．俞兆鹏，李少恒，本卷主编．北京：中华书局，2013．

An Academy Located on Forest and River- Bailudong Academy

The academy (shuyuan) is an ancient Chinese educational institution. Jiangxi is not only the birthplace of ancient Chinese academy culture, but also has the highest number of academies among all provinces in China. According to the statistics of scholars, there were 990 academies in Jiangxi in the past, accounting for about one-seventh of the country's total. The Jiangxi academy was praised by the people of the time for the completeness of its rules and the high quality of its schooling. The Bailudong (White Deer Cave) Academy became the first of the four major academies in China, and others such as the Ehu (Goose Lake) Academy, the Bailu zhou (White Heron) Academy and the Xiangshan Academy were also well known throughout the country.

Founded in the late Tang Dynasty and rebuilt in the Southern Song Dynasty, the Bailudong Academy has a history of more than 1,000 years and is known as "the top school in the world" and "the first school in the world". Famous Confucian scholars such as Zhu Xi, Lu Jiuyuan and Wang Yangming have all taught here.

The reason why the Bailudong Academy has become the top academy in the world is inseparable from Zhu Xi. Zhu Xi put a lot of effort into rebuilding the Bailudong Academy, not only lecturing in person, but also formulating the *Revealing of the Bailudong Academy*, which clarified the purpose of education and set out the basic requirements for cultivating one's moral character, handling one's affairs and receiving things.

The Revealing of the Bailudong Academy became the common school rules followed by all the local academy, and then spread to Korea and Japan during the Ming and Qing dynasties. Korea was deeply influenced by the Chinese academy, and under the influence of the Bailudong Academy, the Baiyundong（White Cloud Cave）Seowon was established. The Baekludong Seowon School Rules are still hung above the lecture halls of Shaosu Seowon（Shaoxiu Academy）and Tausan Seowon（Taoshan Academy）in South Korea. In some Japanese and South Korean country schools, there is still a collective chanting of *The Revealing of the Bailudong Academy*.

第九课　樟树的中药多极了！
LESSON 9 Zhangshu has many traditional Chinese medicines!

- 知识目标：了解并掌握"除了……（以外），都/还/也……"和"形容词/心理动词+极了"的用法
- 能力目标：能够用汉语表达自己的想法和情绪
- 文化目标：了解江西的中药和中医文化

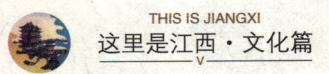

第九课　樟树的中药多极了！

Key Sentences
重点句　Zhòngdiǎn jù

1. 樟树的中药多极了！　　　　　Zhāngshù de zhōngyào duō jí le!
2. 除了历史悠久以外，樟树　　　Chúle lìshǐ yōujiǔ yǐwài, Zhāngshù
   的中药也非常有名。　　　　　de zhōngyào yě fēicháng yǒumíng.

Warm-up
热身　Rèshēn

说一说，关于中药你知道什么？

What do you know about Chinese medicine?

gǒuqǐ
枸杞

chénpí
陈皮

第九课 樟树的中药多极了！
LESSON 9 Zhangshu has many traditional Chinese medicines!

niúhuáng
牛黄

gāncǎo
甘草

huánglián
黄连

dāngguī
当归

Texts
课文 kèwén

A

Měinà: Wáng lǎoshī, wǒmen hái yǒu duō jiǔ dào Zhāngshù?
美娜：王老师，我们还有多久到樟树？

Wáng Yuè: Dàgài hái yǒu wǔ fēnzhōng. Gāotiě hěn kuài.
王月：大概还有五分钟。高铁很快。

Héxī: Shì a, gāotiě kuài jí le!
荷西：是啊，高铁快极了！

Pí'āi'ěr: Gāotiě yòu kuài yòu shūfu. Wǒmen kěyǐ yìbiān zuò gāotiě,
皮埃尔：高铁又快又舒服。我们可以一边坐高铁，
yìbiān kàn fēngjǐng.
一边看风景。

Wáng Yuè: Tóngxué men, dào le Zhāngshù hòu, wǒmen xiān qù bīnguǎn,
王月：同学们，到了樟树后，我们先去宾馆，
ránhòu qù Zhōngyīyào Bówùguǎn.
然后去中医药博物馆。

美娜：Tài hǎo le! Jīntiān kěyǐ kàn dào bùtóng de zhōngyào le.
美娜：太好了！今天可以看到不同的中药了。

荷西：Shì a, wǒ yìzhí xiǎng liáojiě zhōngyào, jīntiān zhōngyú kěyǐ kànkan le.
荷西：是啊，我一直想了解中药，今天终于可以看看了。

皮埃尔：Wǒ gēn nǐ yíyàng, yě duì zhōngyào hěn gǎn xìngqù.
皮埃尔：我跟你一样，也对中药很感兴趣。

王月：Zhāngshù de zhōngyào duō jí le! Dàjiā kěyǐ xué dào hěn duō zhōngyī hé zhōngyào de zhīshi. Mǎshàng dào Zhāngshù le, wǒmen zhǔnbèi xià chē ba.
王月：樟树的中药多极了！大家可以学到很多中医和中药的知识。马上到樟树了，我们准备下车吧。

美娜：Hǎo de.
美娜：好的。

English Version

Mena: How long till we get to Zhangshu, Ms. Wang?

Wang Yue: It's about 5 minutes. The high-speed train is very fast.

Jose: Yes, the high-speed train is really fast! We can take the train and enjoy the scenery at the same time.

Wang Yue: Boys and girls, after we arrived in Zhangshu, we will go to the hotel first and then visit the Traditional Chinese Medicine Museum.

Jose: Great! I always want to know traditional Chinese medicine, finally I have the chance to see it today.

Pierre: Me too, I'm quite interested in traditional Chinese medicines.

第九课　樟树的中药多极了！
LESSON 9 Zhangshu has many traditional Chinese medicines!

Wang Yue: Zhangshu has so many traditional Chinese medicines! We can learn a lot of it. We will soon arrive in Zhangshu, let's get ready to get off.

Mena: Okay.

生词　*New Words*

1.	大概	dàgài	adv.	approximately, about
2.	舒服	shūfu	adj.	comfortable
3.	不同	bùtóng	adj.	different
4.	中药	zhōngyào	n.	traditional Chinese medicine
5.	一直	yìzhí	adv.	all the time, always
6.	终于	zhōngyú	adv.	finally
7.	中医	zhōngyī	n.	traditional Chinese medical therapy
8.	知识	zhīshi	n.	knowledge
9.	马上	mǎshàng	adv.	at once, immediately
10.	准备	zhǔnbèi	v.	to prepare, to set out
11.	下车	xià chē	v.	to get off (from the car, bus, train)

Texts
课文 kèwén

B

Dǎoyóu: Nǐmen hǎo, huānyíng nǐmen lái dào Zhōngyīyào Bówùguǎn! Wǒ shì nǐmen de dǎoyóu, hěn gāoxìng rènshi nǐmen.
导游：你们好，欢迎你们来到中医药博物馆！我是你们的导游，很高兴认识你们。

Měinà: Hěn gāoxìng rènshi nín.
美娜：很高兴认识您。

Dǎoyóu: Zhèlǐ zhǔyào jièshào le zhōngyī hé zhōngyào de lìshǐ, yóuqí shì guānyú Zhāngshù de zhōngyào lìshǐ.
导游：这里主要介绍了中医和中药的历史，尤其是关于樟树的中药历史。

Héxī: Zhāngshù de zhōngyào lìshǐ cháng jí le.
荷西：樟树的中药历史长极了。

Dǎoyóu: Shì de, chú le lìshǐ cháng yǐwài, Zhāngshù de zhōngyào yě fēicháng yǒumíng.
导游：是的，除了历史长以外，樟树的中药也非常有名。

Pí'āi'ěr: Yīnwèi Zhāngshù de zhōngyào yòu hǎo yòu duō, suǒyǐ Zhāngshù yě jiào "yàodū", duì ma?
皮埃尔：因为樟树的中药又好又多，所以樟树也叫"药都"，对吗？

Dǎoyóu: Duì. Nǐmen kàn, zhèxiē dōu shì zhōngyào. Chú le zhèxiē huā hé cǎo yǐwài, yǒuxiē dòngwù yě kěyǐ zuò chéng zhōngyào.
导游：对。你们看，这些都是中药。除了这些花和草以外，有些动物也可以做成中药。

第九课　樟树的中药多极了！
LESSON 9 Zhangshu has many traditional Chinese medicines!

Měinà: Méi xiǎngdào zhèxiē dōu shì zhōngyào.
美娜：没想到这些都是中药。

Dǎoyóu: Chúle jièshào zhōngyào yǐwài, wǒ hái yào gàosu nǐmen zěnme zuò zhōngyào.
导游：除了介绍中药以外，我还要告诉你们怎么做中药。

Héxī: Zhēnde ma? Wǒ xiǎng zhīdào zěnme zuò zhōngyào.
荷西：真的吗？我想知道怎么做中药。

Dǎoyóu: Dāngrán shì zhēnde. Wǒmen zǒu ba, yìqǐ qù nàbian zuò zhōngyào.
导游：当然是真的。我们走吧，一起去那边做中药。

Pí'āi'ěr: Hǎo de.
皮埃尔：好的。

English Version

Tour guide: Hello, welcome to Traditional Chinese medicine Museum! I'm your tour guide, nice to meet you.

Mena: Nice to meet you too.

Tour guide: Here introduces the history of traditional Chinese medicine and traditional Chinese medical therapy, especially the history of Zhangshu's traditional Chinese medicine.

Jose: Zhangshu has a very long history of traditional Chinese medicine.

Tour guide: Yeah, besides the long history, the traditional Chinese medicine of Zhangshu is also very famous.

Pierre: Because Zhangshu has many kinds of traditional Chinese medicines and the quality of medicine is very good, Zhangshu is also called the capital of medicine. Right?

Tour guide: Exactly. You see, these are traditional Chinese medicines. Besides these flowers and grass, some animals also can be made into medicines.

Mena: I never expected these are traditional Chinese medicines.

Tour guide: Besides introducing traditional Chinese medicine, I will also tell you how to make it.

Jose: Really? I want to know how to make it.

Tour guide: Of course. Let's go and make it together over there.

Pierre: OK.

生词 New Words

1. 导游	dǎoyóu	n.	tour guide
2. 认识	rènshi	v.&n.	❶to know; ❷knowledge
3. 介绍	jièshào	v.	to introduce
4. 关于	guānyú	prep.	about
5. 除了	chúle	prep.	besides; except
6. 以外	yǐwài	n.	beyond, except
7. 这些	zhèxiē	pron.	these
8. 有些	yǒuxiē	pron.	some
9. 动物	dòngwù	n.	animal
10. 成	chéng	v.	to become
11. 告诉	gàosu	v.	to tell

Proper Noun
专有名词 Zhuānyǒu míngcí

樟树	Zhāngshù	Zhangshu City, a city in Jiangxi
中医药博物馆	Zhōngyīyào Bówùguǎn	Traditional Chinese Medicine Museum

Grammar
语法 Yǔfǎ

1. 程度的表达：极了 "极了"Indicates Degree

"形容词/心理动词+极了"表示最高程度。

"Adj./Mental Verb+ 极了" express the superlative degree.

（1）樟树的中药多极了！

（2）今天南昌热极了！

（3）这个地方我喜欢极了！

2. 除了……（以外），都/还/也…… The Structure "除了……以外，都/还/也……"

"除了……（以外），都/还/也……"表示排除特殊，其他的都是相同的情况。它还表示排除已经知道的，后面补充其他的信息。

"除了……（以外），都/还/也……" used to exclude the special case, and the rest has the same situation. It also can be used to exclude the items that we already known and add other information.

（1）除了老师（以外），我们都不是中国人。

（2）除了江西（以外），其他地方我都没去过。

（4）除了介绍中药（以外），我还要告诉你们怎么做中药。

（5）除了历史悠久（以外），樟树的中药也非常有名。

1. 根据课文回答问题　Answer the questions according to the texts

（1）高铁怎么样？

（2）哪儿的中药多极了？

（3）为什么樟树也叫"药都"？

（4）哪些东西可以做成中药？

（5）樟树的中药历史长吗？

2. 选词填空　Choose the appropriate words to fill in the blanks

　　大概　　舒服　　终于　　没想到　　告诉

（1）_____需要30分钟。

（2）他没_____我。

（3）我们_____做完了这些中药。

（4）高铁又快又_____。

（5）_____中药的历史这么长。

3. 根据所给的词完成句子　Complete the sentences with the given words

（1）_____，他还去过樟树。（除了）

（2）这件衣服_____。（极了）

（3）除了他以外，_____。（都）

（4）除了汉语，_____。（也）

4. 组词成句　Make up sentences with the given words

（1）在　　下车　　哪儿　　我们

_____

（2）极了　　多　　樟树　　中药　　的

_____

（3）他　　去过　　没　　没想到　　中医药博物馆

_____

（4）一直　　想去　　他　　江西　　旅游

_____

5. 交际练习　Communication task

请上网查一查中药的相关知识，说一说你的认识。

Look up the introduction of traditional Chinese medicine, and tell each other what you know.

_____
_____
_____
_____
_____
_____

Cultural Tip
文化贴士　Wénhuà tiēshì

中华药都——樟树

中国的医学有数千年的历史，中医中药不仅是医学技术，也是中华文化的重要组成部分。中国历史悠久，地大物博，药材资源十分丰富。

有"中国药都"之称的樟树市位于江西省中部，因树而得名，因药而扬名。樟树药文化积淀深厚，不仅是药材贸易的集散地，更是药物制作加工的中心，享有"药不到樟树不齐，药不过樟树不灵"之美誉。

樟树药业始于汉晋，成于唐宋，盛于明清，历1800余年不衰，以药材炮制技艺精妙著称于世。东汉建安七年（公元202年），著名丹术家、道教始祖葛玄在阁皂山采药行医、筑灶炼丹，开樟树药业先河。三国时期樟树摆有药摊，唐代设有药墟，宋代形成药市，明清成为南北药材总汇的"药码头"。至清乾隆年间，樟树人开的药店遍布全国，成为国内药界名声大噪的"樟树药帮"。进行药材交易之余，每个药市都形成了各自的交易规则、药市民俗，包括祭祀礼仪和戏曲演出、游艺活动等，吸引了交易者以外的广大民众参与和观赏。

自公元1958年起，樟树每年都会举行全国药材药品交易会，参与地域之广，来者之众，成交品种、金额之多，为全国药材市场之最。时至今日，药业仍是樟树经济发展的支柱产业之一。

Traditional Chinese Medicine Capital – Zhang Shu

China has a long history and vast territory with abundant medicinal resources. Traditional Chinese Medicine (TCM) has a history of thousands years and it is not only a medical technique but also an important part of Chinese culture.

The city of Zhangshu, known as the "Traditional Chinese Medicine Capital", is located in the middle of Jiangxi Province. It is named for its representative trees, Camphor Tree, and famous for its medicine resources. Zhangshu's medicine culture is deep-rooted. It is not only a distribution centre for the trade of medicinal herbs, but also a centre for the production and processing of medicines, and enjoys the reputation of "the quality and quantity of medicine is closely related to Zhangshu".

The industry of medicine in Zhangshu started in the Han and Jin dynasties, became popular in the Tang and Song dynasties, and flourished in the Ming and Qing dynasties, and has been flourished for more than 1800 years. In the 7th year of Jian'an period in the Eastern Han Dynasty (202 AD), Ge Xuan, a famous elixir artist and the founder of Taoism, collected herbs and practiced medicine and built a stove to refine pills in Mount Getsum, opening up the pioneer of Zhangshu medicine. During the Three Kingdoms period, there were medicine stalls in Zhangshu. A small medicine market was set up in the Tang Dynasty, a formal medicine market was formed in the Song Dynasty, and in the Ming and Qing Dynasties, it became a "medicine dock" where medicine materials from the north and the south converged. During the Qianlong period of the Qing Dynasty, Zhangshu people opened pharmacies all over the country and became the "Zhangshu Medicine Gang", which became famous all over the country. In addition to trading herbs, each medicine market developed its own trading rules and folklore, including rituals, opera performances and entertainment, which attracted the participation and enjoyment of the general public outside the traders.

Since 1958, Zhangshu has held a national herbal medicine fair every year, with the widest participation in the region, the largest number of visitors, the largest number of varieties and amounts of money traded, of any herbal market in the country. To this day, the pharmaceutical industry is still one of the pillars of Zhangshu's economic development.

第十课　我被客家文化吸引了
LESSON 10　I am attracted by Hakka culture

- 知识目标：掌握"被"字句以及"如果……（的话），就……"假设句的用法
- 能力目标：能够使用假设句表达观点或想法
- 文化目标：了解客家文化

第十课　我被客家文化吸引了

Key Sentences
重点句　Zhòngdiǎn jù

1. 这个院子被这些房子围在中间。
   Zhè gè yuànzi bèi zhèixiē fángzi wéi zài zhōngjiān.
2. 我被这些漂亮的客家围屋吸引了。
   Wǒ bèi zhèxiē piàoliang de Kèjiā wéiwū xīyǐn le.
3. 如果你喜欢的话，就可以参加。
   Rúguǒ nǐ xǐhuān de huà, jiù kěyǐ cānjiā.

Warm-up
热身　Rèshēn

说一说，关于客家你知道什么？

What do you know about Hakka?

Kèjiā Wéiwū
客家　围屋

Kèjiā Léichá
客家　擂茶

第十课 我被客家文化吸引了
LESSON 10 I am attracted by Hakka culture

Kèjiā cháguǒ
客家 茶果

Kèjiā hànjù
客家 汉剧

Kèjiā wǔdǎo
客家 舞蹈

Kèjiā wǔhuǒlóng
客家 舞火龙

Texts
课文 kèwén

Wáng Yuè: Tóngxuémen, zhèli jiù shì Lóngnán, huānyíng dàjiā lái dào
王 月：同学们，这里 就 是 龙南，欢迎 大家 来 到
zhèli. Wǒmen yìqǐ liǎojiě yíxià Kèjiā wénhuà ba.
这里。我们 一起 了解 一下 客家 文化 吧。

Héxī: Wā, zhèli de fángzi zhēn piàoliang!
荷西：哇，这里 的 房子 真 漂亮！

Měinà: Shì a, yě hěn tèbié, gēn qítā fángzi bù yíyàng.
美娜：是 啊，也 很 特别，跟 其他 房子 不 一样。

Wáng Yuè: Shì de, zhè shì Kèjiā Wéiwū, yě shì yǐqián de lǎo fángzi.
王 月：是的，这 是 客家 围屋，也 是 以前 的 老 房子。

Héxī: Zhè ge fángzi tèbié dà, yǒu sān céng, hái yǒu hěnduō fángjiān.
荷西：这 个 房子 特别 大，有 三 层，还 有 很多 房间。

Měinà: Tā de zhōngjiān shì ge hěn dà de yuànzi.
美娜：它 的 中间 是 个 很 大 的 院子。

Wáng Yuè: Duì, Zhè ge yuànzi bèi zhèxiē fángzi wéi zài zhōngjiān.
王月：对，这个院子被这些房子围在中间。

Héxī: Shì bu shì hěn duō rén zhù zài zhèli ya?
荷西：是不是很多人住在这里呀？

Wáng Yuè: Yǐqián yǒu hěn duō rén zhù zài zhèli, xiànzài tāmen dōu bān qù le chéngshì.
王月：以前有很多人住在这里，现在他们都搬去了城市。

Měinà: Wǒ juéde zhù zài zhèli yídìng fēicháng shūfu.
美娜：我觉得住在这里一定非常舒服。

Wáng Yuè: Shì de, zhù zài zhèli hěn shūfu, dōngtiān bù lěng, xiàtiān bú rè.
王月：是的，住在这里很舒服，冬天不冷，夏天不热。

Héxī: Wǒ bèi zhèxiē Kèjiā Wéiwū xīyǐn le.
荷西：我被这些客家围屋吸引了。

Měinà: Wǒ yě shì, wǒ hěn xiǎng zài zhèli zhù yí duàn shíjiān.
美娜：我也是，我很想在这里住一段时间。

English Version

Wang Yue: Boys and girls, this is Longnan, south Jiangxi. Welcome. Let's learn about Hakka culture together.

Jose: Wow, the houses here are so beautiful!

Mena: Yes, also very special. They're different from other houses.

Wang Yue: Yes, these are Hakka walled villages, which also are the old house in past.

Jose: This house is very big. It has three floors with many rooms.

Mena: The inside part of it is a courtyard.

Wang Yue: Yes, the courtyard is surrounded by these houses.

Jose: Are there many people living here?

第十课　我被客家文化吸引了
LESSON 10 I am attracted by Hakka culture

Wang Yue: A lot of people used to live here, they all move to the city now.

Mena: I think it must be very comfortable to live here.

Wang Yue: Yes, it is. It is not cold in winter and not hot in summer.

Jose: I am attracted by these Hakka walled villages.

Mena: Me too, I would like to stay here for a while.

生词　*New Words*

1.	其他	qítā	pron.	other
2.	房子	fángzi	n.	house
3.	院子	yuànzi	n.	courtyard
4.	被	bèi	prep.	be made or forced, indicating passive voice
5.	围	wéi	v.	to surround
6.	中间	zhōngjiān	n.	middle
7.	搬	bān	v.	to move
8.	城市	chéngshì	n.	city
9.	吸引	xīyǐn	v.	to attract
10.	段	duàn	m.	a measure word for time

Texts 课文 kèwén

王月: 我们刚才看了客家采茶戏,大家觉得怎么样?

荷西: 我觉得很不错!

美娜: 是的,我们都被它吸引了。

王月: 现在我们一起去喝茶,吃客家美食。

荷西: 太好了!

荷西: 王老师,这是什么茶呀?它跟其他茶不一样。

王月: 是的,这叫客家擂茶。除了茶叶,里面还加了其他食物,很好喝,你们尝尝。

美娜: 哇,不错,真好喝。如果可以买到的话,我就买一些,让我的家人和朋友尝尝。

第十课 我被客家文化吸引了
LESSON 10 I am attracted by Hakka culture

Wáng Yuè: Wǒmen kěyǐ yìqǐ zài zhèli chī wǎnfàn, cháng yí xià Kèjiā měishí.
王 月：我们 可以 一起 在 这里 吃 晚饭，尝 一 下 客家 美食。
　　　　Wǎnshang hái yǒu Kèjiā wǔdǎo biǎoyǎn.
　　　　晚上 还 有 客家 舞蹈 表演。

Héxī: Tài hǎo le! Wǒ kěyǐ hé tāmen yìqǐ tiàowǔ ma?
荷西：太 好 了！我 可以 和 他们 一起 跳舞 吗？

Wáng Yuè: Rúguǒ nǐ xǐhuan de huà, jiù kěyǐ cānjiā.
王 月：如果 你 喜欢 的 话，就 可以 参加。

Héxī: Xièxie lǎoshī, wǒ yídìng cānjiā.
荷西：谢谢 老师，我 一定 参加。

Měinà: Tài hǎo le, wǒ yě yào cānjiā.
美娜：太 好 了，我 也 要 参加。

English Version

Wang Yue: We just watched the Hakka Tea-picking show, how do you like it?

Jose: I think it's pretty good!

Mena: Yes, we were all attracted by it.

Wang Yue: Now let's go to drink tea and eat Hakka food.

Jose: Great!

Jose: Ms. Wang, what kind of tea is this? It is different from other teas.

Wang Yue: Yes, this is called Hakka Grounded tea. Besides the tea leaves, there are other foods in it, it's delicious, you can try it.

Mena: Wow, nice! It's really delicious. If I can get some, I'll buy some for my family and friends to try.

Wang Yue: We can have dinner here and taste Hakka food. There is also a Hakka dance performance in the evening.

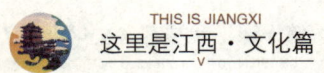

Jose: Great! Can I join the dance?

Wang Yue: If you like, you can participate.

Jose: Thank you, Ms. Wang, I will definitely participate.

Mena: Great, I want to participate too.

生词 New Words

1.	刚才	gāngcái	n.	just now
2.	尝	cháng	v.	to taste
3.	不错	bùcuò	adj.	pretty good
4.	美食	měishí	n.	delicacy
5.	茶叶	cháyè	n.	tea leaves
6.	如果	rúguǒ	conj.	if
7.	让	ràng	v.	to let
8.	舞蹈	wǔdǎo	n.	dance
9.	参加	cānjiā	v.	to join, to participate

Proper Noun
专有名词 Zhuānyǒu míngcí

龙南	Longnán	a county town in Jiangxi Province
客家	Kèjiā	Hakka
围屋	Wéiwū	Hakka walled village
擂茶	Léichá	Grounded Tea

Grammar 语法 Yǔfǎ

1. "被" 字句　A sentence with "被"

"被"字句表示被动的意义,句子结构为"主语+被+(宾语)+动词+其他"。在否定句式中,否定副词放在"被"字前面。

A sentence with "被" expresses the passive meaning, the structure of the sentence is "S+ 被 +O+Verb+Other Elements". The negative adverb should be put before "被" in negative sentences.

（1）咖啡被美娜喝了。

（2）面包(miàn bāo)(bread)被她吃了。

（3）那个房间没被预订。

（4）书没被她拿走。

2. "如果……(的话),就……"　The Structure of Conjunction: "如果……(的话),就……"

这个连词结构由两个分句组成,第一个分句"如果……(的话)"表示假设,第二个分句"就……"表示在第一个分句发生的情况下产生的结果。第一个分句的"的话"可以省略,如果两个分句的主语是同一个,主语可以省略。

The structure is composed by two causes, the first cause with "如果" is a hypothesis, the second cause with "就" is the result based on the hypothesis. The words "的话" can be omitted, and the subject should be put at the front of the second cause, and it can also be omitted.

（1）如果你喜欢（的话），就买一件。

（2）如果你渴（的话），就喝点儿水。

（3）如果你有时间（的话），就可以参加。

1. 根据课文回答下面的问题　Answer the questions according to the texts

（1）客家围屋有什么特点？

（2）荷西觉得客家采茶戏怎么样？

（3）现在有很多人住在客家围屋里吗？

（4）王月老师和荷西、美娜都做了什么？

2. 选词填空　Choose the appropriate words to fill in the blanks

　　吸引　　如果　　不错　　刚才　　搬

（1）_____你喜欢的话，就可以参加这个表演。

（2）我们都被客家围屋_____了。

（3）这些食物很_____。

（4）他们都_____去了城市。

（5）我们_____看了客家采茶戏。

3. 替换练习　Substitution drills

（1）A: 哇，<u>这里</u>的<u>房子</u>真<u>漂亮</u>！

　　　B: 是呀，跟其他<u>房子</u>不一样。

　　南昌　　好玩　　城市

江西的春天　　舒服　　地方

客家舞蹈　　特别　　舞蹈

（2）如果<u>可以买到</u>的话，我就<u>买一些</u>。

可以去　　明天去那里

可以借　　借这本书

能坐飞机　　坐飞机

（3）我们<u>被客家文化吸引</u>了。

蛋糕　　弟弟吃完

那本书　　她拿走

那杯茶　　他喝完

4. 组词成句　Make up sentences with the given words

（1）我　被　电影　这个　了　吸引

_____

（2）江西的　觉得　风景　我　很不错

_____

（3）想　在这儿　住　他　一段时间

_____

（4）南昌　一个　是　城市　很漂亮的

_____

（5）这里　晚上　有　表演　舞蹈

_____

5. 交际练习　Communication Task

请用汉语跟你的朋友介绍客家文化

Please introduce Hakka culture to your friend in Chinese.

Cultural Tip
文化贴士　Wénhuà tiēshì

古代汉文化活化石——客家文化

客家是中国汉民族中的一个稳定而又独特的民系,由不同历史时期迁徙到南方的中原人组成。江西省南部的赣州市是客家人南迁第一站,也是客家人的主要居住地之一,客家人占赣州市全市人口的95%以上[①]。

随着客家人在赣南定居,古代中原文化与原住民文化结合,形成具有特色的赣南客家文化,主要体现在建筑、饮食、民俗、方言等方面。

在建筑方面,客家的民居往往保留着中原特征,门榜或者牌匾上,往往写着家族的堂号、姓氏源流。围屋也是客家建筑的特色,赣南的客家围屋多为方形,与福建的圆形土楼和广东的围龙屋呈现出不同的风格。

---
① 数据来自赣州市人民政府官方网站

在饮食方面，赣南客家饮食以咸辣为主，特色菜有菜干扣肉、粉蒸肉、三杯鸡等；客家米酒、擂茶也很有名。

在民俗方面，赣南采茶戏、客家山歌、上犹县"九狮拜象"、宁都县"竹篙火龙"等都是赣南客家的特色。

在方言方面，客家话是客家人最显著的标志之一，客家方言中保留了中原正音和大量古汉语，被称为古汉语的"活化石"。

客家人在不断的南迁过程中，有的扎根异乡，有的远渡重洋，但他们一直保持着高度的凝聚力和向心力。奋发进取、团结和睦的精神既是中华优秀传统文化的精华，也是客家精神的典型体现。

Hakka Culture, a living fossil of ancient Han culture

The Hakka are a stable and distinctive people group among China's Han people, consisting of people from the Central Plains who migrated to the South at different times in history. The city of Ganzhou in southern Jiangxi Province was the first stop of the Hakka migration to the South and is one of the main settlements of the Hakka people, who make up more than 95% of the city's population.

As the Hakka settled in Gannan, the ancient Central Plains culture combined with the aboriginal culture to form the distinctive Gannan Hakka culture, which is mainly reflected in architecture, food, folklore and dialects.

In terms of architecture, Hakka dwellings often retain the characteristics of the Middle Kingdom, with door lists or plaques often bearing the family hall name and the origin of the family name. The enclosed houses are also characteristic of Hakka architecture. Hakka enclosed houses in Gannan are mostly square in shape, showing a different style from the rounded earthen buildings in Fujian and the enclosed dragon houses in Guangdong.

In terms of food, the Hakka diet in Gannan is mainly salty and spicy, with specialties such as dried and buttoned pork, steamed pork and three cups of chicken; Hakka rice wine and ringed tea are also famous.

In terms of folklore, the Gannan Hakka tea opera, Hakka mountain songs, the "nine lions worshipping the elephant" in Shangyou County and the "Penny Fire Dragon" in Ningdu County are all special features of the Hakka people of Gannan.

In terms of dialect, the Hakka dialect is one of the most distinctive features of the Hakka people. It is known as a living fossil of the ancient Chinese language, as it retains the orthography of the Central Plains and a large number of ancient Chinese characters.

The Hakka people have continued to migrate southwards, some with roots in foreign lands and some across the ocean, but they have always maintained a high degree of cohesion and centripetal force. The spirit of enterprise, unity and harmony is the essence of the excellent traditional Chinese culture and a typical embodiment of the Hakka spirit.

生词总表 VOCABULARY

生词 New Words

词 Word	拼音 Pinyin	词类 Parts of Speech	词义 Meaning	课号 Lesson
A				
安静	ānjìng	n.	quiet	L8
B				
把	bǎ	prep.	(used in the "把" sentence) denoting the disposal of something	L7
搬	bān	v.	to move	L10
包	bāo	v.	to wrap up	L2
杯	bēi	m.&n.	❶a cup of; ❷cup	L1
被	bèi	prep.	be made or forced, indicating passive voice	L10
闭	bì	v.	to close, to shut	L7
变	biàn	v.	to change	L3
表演	biǎoyǎn	n.	performance	L6
别	bié	adv.	don't	L7
比如	bǐrú	v.	for example	L6
不错	bùcuò	adj.	pretty good	L10
不同	bùtóng	adj	different	L9
C				
采	cǎi	v.	to pick	L6
菜	cài	n.	❶dish; ❷vegetable	L1
菜单	càidān	n.	menu	L1
餐	cān	n.	meal, food	L1
参观	cānguān	v.	to visit	L4

词 Word	拼音 Pinyin	词类 Parts of Speech	词义 Meaning	课号 Lesson
参加	cānjiā	v.	join, participate	L10
草	cǎo	n.	grass	L7
层	céng	m.	floor	L3
曾经	céngjīng	adv.	ever; once	L8
茶杯	chábēi	n.	teacup	L2
茶叶	cháyè	n.	tea leaves	L10
长	cháng	adj.	long	L5
成	chéng	v.	to become	L9
城市	chéngshì	n.	city	L10
除了	chúle	prep.	besides; except	L9
瓷器	cíqì	n.	porcelain	L2
D					
打车	dǎchē	v.	to take a taxi	L3
大概	dàgài	adv.	approximately, about	L9
带	dài	v.	to carry; to take; to bring;	L2
但是	dànshì	conj.	but, still, yet	L1
当然	dāngrán	adv.	of course; certainly	L6
导游	dǎoyóu	n.	tour guide	L9
等	děng	part.	and so on	L5
点	diǎn	v.	to select from many things	L1
电梯	diàntī	n.	elevator	L3
地方	dìfang	n.	place	L5
懂	dǒng	v.	to understand, to know	L6
动物	dòngwù	n.	animal	L9
对	duì	prep.&adj.	❶（used before a noun or pronoun）to, for; ❷right	L8
E					
饿	è	adj.	be hungry	L1

词 Word	拼音 Pinyin	词类 Parts of Speech	词义 Meaning	课号 Lesson
F				
房子	fángzi	n.	house	L10
放	fàng	v.	to put	L7
放假	fàng jià	v.	to have a holiday or vacation	L2
饭馆	fànguǎn	n.	restaurant	L1
份	fèn	m.	a set of	L1
风景	fēngjǐng	n.	scenery, landscape	L3
G				
感兴趣	gǎn xìngqù		to be interested in	L8
刚才	gāngcái	n.	just now	L10
告诉	gàosu	v.	to tell	L9
跟	gēn	prep.	with	L6
更	gèng	adv.	more, even more	L5
各式各样	gèshìgèyàng	idm.	all kinds of	L4
工具	gōngjù	n.	tool	L4
关于	guānyú	prep.	about	L9
逛	guàng	v.	to stroll, to wander	L7
古代	gǔdài	n.	ancient times	L7
孤独	gūdú	adj.	lonely	L7
柜子	guìzi	n.	cupboard, cabinet	L7
过	guo	part.	used after a verb to indicate the completion of an action	L1
果汁	guǒzhī	n.	fruit juice	L1
国家	guójiā	n.	country, nation	L6
H				
好看	hǎokàn	adj.	beautiful	L2
喝	hē	v.	to drink	L5

词 Word	拼音 Pinyin	词类 Parts of Speech	词义 Meaning	课号 Lesson
画	huà	v.&n.	to paint; painting	L4
画家	huàjiā	n.	painter	L7
环境	huánjìng	n.	environment	L8
皇帝	huángdì	n.	emperor	L2
或者	huòzhě	conj.	or	L1
J				
机会	jīhuì	n.	chance; opportunity	L5
记得	jìde	v.	to remember	L7
坚持	jiānchí	v.	to persist in, to insist on	L6
简单	jiǎndān	adj.	easy; simple	L2
见	jiàn	v.	to see	L3
建筑	jiànzhù	n.	architecture	L8
讲课	jiǎng kè	v.	to give a lecture	L8
加油	jiāyóu	v.	to cheer	L6
教	jiāo	v.	to teach	L2
骄傲	jiāo'ào	adj.	pride, proud	L7
脚	jiǎo	n.	the foot of a hill or mountain	L8
介绍	jièshào	v.	to introduce	L9
进	jìn	v.	to enter	L3
久	jiǔ	adj.	long, long time	L3
K				
开心	kāixīn	adj.	happy, joyous	L5
看起来	kànqǐlái	v.	to look like	L10
空气	kōngqì	n.	air; atmosphere	L8
口袋	kǒudài	n.	pocket	L7
快	kuài	adv.	quickly	L8
L				
里	lǐ	n.	inside	L7

词 Word	拼音 Pinyin	词类 Parts of Speech	词义 Meaning	课号 Lesson
聊天儿	liáotiānr	v.	to chat	L5
了解	liǎojiě	v.	to know	L5
里边	lǐbian	n.	inside	L1
厉害	lìhai	adj	terrific; extraordinary	L4
历史	lìshǐ	n.	history	L4
楼	lóu	n.	building, floor	L3
楼上	lóushang	n.	upstairs	L3
楼梯	lóutī	n.	stairs	L3
录	lù	v.	to record	L4
		M		
马上	mǎshàng	adv.	at once, immediately	L9
毛笔	máobǐ	n.	writing brush	L4
美食	měishí	n.	delicacy	L10
门口	ménkǒu	n.	entrance	L3
米	mǐ	m.	meter	L3
墨水	mòshuǐ	n.	ink	L4
		N		
耐心	nàixīn	n.	patience	L4
年	nián	n.	year	L4
鸟	niǎo	n.	bird	L7
		P		
陪	péi	v.	to accompany	L8
瓶	píng	m.	bottle	L4
		Q		
其他	qítā	pron.	other	L10
千	qiān	m.	thousand	L4
其中	qízhōng	n.	among	L8

词 Word	拼音 Pinyin	词类 Parts of Speech	词义 Meaning	课号 Lesson
R				
让	ràng	v.	to let	L10
人们	rénmen	n.	people	L6
认识	rènshi	v.& n.	❶to know; ❷knowledge	L9
人物	rénwù	n.	figure	L8
如果……就……	rúguǒ……jiù……	conj.	if...then	L10
S				
扫	sǎo	v.	❶to scan; ❷sweep	L1
省	shěng	n.	province	L8
师傅	shīfù	n.	master worker (a qualified worker as distinct from an apprentice)	L2
试	shì	v.	to try	L2
市	shì	n.	city	L8
视频	shìpín	n.	video	L4
石头	shítou	n.	stone	L7
书法	shūfǎ	n.	calligraphy	L4
舒服	shūfu	adj	comfortable	L9
树	shù	n.	tree	L7
水	shuǐ	n.	water	L7
虽然	suīrán	conj.	although, though	L6
所以	suǒyǐ	conj.	so, therefore	L5
T				
太	tài	adv.	too, excessively	L5
趟	tàng	m.	used for a round trip, etc.	L5
特别	tèbié	adj. &adv.	❶special; ❷very	L6
特色	tèsè	n.	salient feature	L1
听说	tīngshuō	v.	to hear of	L1

词 Word	拼 音 Pinyin	词 类 Parts of Speech	词 义 Meaning	课 号 Lesson
W					
哇	wā	int.	wow	L2
完	wán	v.	to finish	L7
碗	wǎn	m.&n.	❶a bowl of; ❷bowl	L1
围	wéi	v.	to surround	L10
位	wèi	m.	a respectful measure word for people	L1
文化	wénhuà	n.	culture	L8
舞蹈	wǔdǎo	n.	dance	L10
X				
吸引	xīyǐn	v.	to attract	L10
习惯	xíguàn	v.&n.	❶to be accustomed to; ❷habit	L1
戏曲	xìqǔ	n.	traditional（Chinese）opera	L5
下车	xià chē	v.	to get off（from the car, bus, train）	L9
现金	xiànjīn	n.	cash	L4
小票	xiǎopiào	n.	receipt	L4
小时候	xiǎoshíhou	n.	in one's childhood	L3
写	xiě	v.	to write	L4
新鲜	xīnxiān	adj.	fresh	L8
休闲	xiūxián	v.	relax	L5
需要	xūyào	v.	need	L4
学者	xuézhě	n.	scholar	L8
Y				
颜料	yánliào	n.	pigment	L4
眼睛	yǎnjing	n.	eye	L7
衣服	yīfu	n.	clothes	L6
一定	yídìng	adv.	definitely	L4
一样	yíyàng	adj.	same, as...as...	L6

词 Word	拼音 Pinyin	词类 Parts of Speech	词义 Meaning	课号 Lesson
以后	yǐhòu	n.	afterwards, later	L2
已经	yǐjīng	adv.	already	L3
以前	yǐqián	adv.	before; previous	L2
以外	yǐwài	n.	Beyond; except	L9
一边	yìbiān	adv.	indicating two actions taking place at the same time	L5
一点儿	yìdiǎnr	num.&m.	a few, a little	L5
一直	yìzhí	adv.	all the time, always	L9
因为	yīnwèi	conj.	because	L5
悠久	yōujiǔ	adj.	long	L4
有点儿	yǒudiǎnr	adv.	a bit, a little, slightly	L1
有关	yǒuguān	v.	to be relevant, about	L8
有名	yǒumíng	adj.	famous	L3
又	yòu	adv.	again	L5
有些	yǒu xiē	pron.	some	L9
院子	yuànzi	n.	courtyard	L10
越	yuè	adv.	more, to a greater degree	L6
Z				
着急	zháojí	adj.	worry, anxious	L7
这么	zhème	adv.	so, such	L3
这些	zhè xiē	pron.	these	L9
支	zhī	m.	a measure word used with long, stick-like objects	L4
知道	zhīdào	v.	to know	L6
支付	zhīfù	v.	pay	L4
知识	zhīshi	n.	knowledge	L9
中药	zhōngyào	n.	Traditional Chinese medicine	L9
中医	zhōngyī	n.	Traditional Chinese medical therapy	L9

词 Word	拼音 Pinyin	词类 Parts of Speech	词义 Meaning	课号 Lesson
终于	zhōngyú	adv.	finally	L9
种类	zhǒnglèi	n.	kind, variety	L6
种	zhòng	v.	to plant	L5
周末	zhōumò	n.	weekend	L3
专门	zhuānmén	adj.&adv.	❶special; specialized; ❷specially	L2
转	zhuàn	v.	to turn; to revolve	L2
准备	zhǔnbèi	v.	to prepare, to set out	L9
自行车	zìxíngchē	n.	bicycle	L1
走路	zǒulù	v.	to walk	L1
最近	zuìjìn	adv.	lately, recently	L6
左右	zuǒyòu	n.	(used after a numeral) about; around	L8
做	zuò	v.	to make; to produce	L2

专有名词 *Proper Noun*

词 Word	拼音 Pinyin	词类 Parts of Speech	词义 Meaning	
B				
八大山人	Bādàshānrén	a famous painter in Ming Dynasty	L7
C				
采茶戏	Cǎicháxì	Tea-picking Opera	L6
G				
赣江	Gànjiāng	Gan River, a branch of the Yangtze River	L3
赣剧	Gànjù	Gan Opera	L6
赣南	Gànnán	southern Jiangxi	L10

词 Word	拼 音 Pinyin	词 类 Parts of Speech	词 义 Meaning
J			
景德镇浮梁茶	Jǐngdézhèn Fúliángchá	Jingdezhen Fuliang Tea	L5
京剧	Jīngjù	Beijing Opera	L6
K			
客家	Kèjiā	Hakka	L10
客家擂茶	Kèjiā léichá	Hakka Lei tea	L10
客家酿豆腐	Kèjiā niàngdòufu	Hakka Meat-Stuffed Tofu	L1
L			
莲花血鸭	Liánhuā xuěyā	Lianhua Braised Duck	L1
庐山云雾茶	Lúshān Yúnwùchá	Lushan Yunwu (Cloud and Mist) Tea	L5
M			
明伦堂	Mínglún Táng	Minglun Hall	L8
N			
南宋	Nán Sòng	the Southern Song Dynasty (1127-1279)	L8
S			
三杯鸡	Sānbēijī	Stewed Chicken with Three Cups of Sauce	L1
思贤台	Sīxián Tái	Sixian Terrace	L8
遂川狗牯脑茶	Suìchuān Gǒugǔnǎochá	Suichuan gougunao Tea	L5
W			
文港	Wéngǎng	Wengang Town, a town in Jiangxi	L4
婺源绿茶	Wùyuán Lùchá	Wuyuan green Tea	L5
X			
修水宁红茶	Xiūshuǐ Nínghóngchá	Xiushui Ning-Black Tea	L5

词 Word	拼 音 Pinyin	词 类 Parts of Speech	词 义 Meaning
Y			
弋阳腔	Yìyángqiāng	Yiyang Opera; Yiyang Tune	L6
御书阁	Yùshū Gé	Yushu Pavilion	L8
御窑厂	Yùyáo Chǎng	Imperial Kiln Factory	L2
Z			
樟树	Zhāngshù	Zhangshu City	L9
中医药博物馆	Zhōngyīyào Bówùguǎn	Traditional Chinese Medicine Museum	L9
朱熹	Zhū Xī	a philosopher in the Southern Song Dynasty	L8
朱子祠	Zhūzǐ Cí	Zhuzi Memorial Temple	L8

参考书目 BIBLIOGRAPHY

1. 黄明亮, 万剑敏, 喻峰. 趣闻江西 [M]. 北京：旅游教育出版社, 2006.

2. 周文英等. 中国地域文化丛书：江西文化 [M]. 沈阳：辽宁教育出版社, 1993.

3. 政协江西省景德镇市委员会. 景德镇文化研究 [M]. 北京：中国文史出版社, 2018.

4. 俞兆鹏, 李少恒. 中国地域文化通览：江西卷 [M]// 中袁行霈, 陈进玉. 中国地域文化通览. 北京：中华书局, 2013.

5. 刘祯. 中国戏曲艺术与地方文化丛书 [M]. 南京：江苏人民出版社, 2020.

6. 《中国戏曲音乐集成》编辑委员会, 《中国戏曲音乐集成·江西卷》编辑委员会. 中国戏曲音乐集成：江西卷（上、下）[M]. 北京：中国 ISBN 中心, 1999.

7. 郑国珍, 姚糖, 蔡晴, 王锦海. 中国古建筑文化之旅：福建·江西 [M]. 北京：知识产权出版社, 2002.

8. 丘桓兴. 客家人与客家文化 [M]. 北京：中国国际广播出版社, 2011.